READING AND VOCABULARY
Focus

Jessica Williams

Series Consultant
Lawrence J. Zwier

NATIONAL GEOGRAPHIC LEARNING | CENGAGE Learning

Australia • Brazil • Japan • Korea • Mexico • Singapore • Spain • United Kingdom • United States

Reading and Vocabulary Focus 3

Jessica Williams

Publisher: Sherrise Roehr

Series Consultant: Lawrence J. Zwier

Executive Editor: Laura Le Dréan

Contributing Editors: Bernard Seal and
Jennifer Bixby

Director of Global Marketing: Ian Martin

International Marketing Manager: Caitlin Thomas

Director, Content and Media Production:
Michael Burggren

Senior Content Project Manager: Daisy Sosa

Print Buyer: Mary Beth Hennebury

Cover Designers: Christopher Roy and
Michael Rosenquest

Cover Image: GARDEL Bertrand/hemis.fr/Getty
Images

Text Design and Layout: Don Williams

Composition: Page Designs International

For product information and technology assistance, contact us at
**Cengage Learning Customer & Sales Support,
1-800-354-9706**

For permission to use material from this text or product,
submit all requests online at **www.cengage.com/permissions**.
Further permissions questions can be e-mailed to
permissionrequest@cengage.com.

Student Book ISBN: 978-1-285-17336-8

National Geographic Learning
20 Channel Center Street
Boston, MA 02210
USA

Cengage Learning is a leading provider of customized learning solutions with office locations around the globe, including Singapore, the United Kingdom, Australia, Mexico, Brazil and Japan.

Cengage Learning products are represented in Canada by Nelson Education, Ltd.

Visit National Geographic Learning online at **ngl.cengage.com**

Visit our corporate website at **www.cengage.com**

Printed in the United States of America
3 4 5 6 7 8   19 18 17 16 15 14

CONTENTS

Inside a Unit   vi

Series Introduction   xi

THE BODY IN MOTION   2

READING 1   **A Natural Way to Run**   4

    READING SKILL: Connecting Visual
Materials to a Text   10

READING 2   **The Runner's High**   14

    READING SKILL: Connecting Ideas with
Signal Words: *this*, *these*, and *such*   18

UNIT REVIEW   22

ONE

TIME   24

READING 1   **Spring Forward, Fall Back**   26

    READING SKILL: Understanding the
Writer's Perspective   32

READING 2   **In Search of an Accurate Calendar**   36

    READING SKILL: Creating Time Lines   42

UNIT REVIEW   46

TWO

WATER   48

READING 1   **Drinking Water**   50

    READING SKILL: Recognizing Implicit
Conditions   56

READING 2   **The Bottled-Water Debate**   60

    READING SKILL: Supporting Details in a
Persuasive Text   64

UNIT REVIEW   68

THREE

CONTENTS (CONTINUED)

FOUR TRAVEL 70

READING 1   **Extreme Diving** 72

READING SKILL: Finding Out Why 78

READING 2   **Disaster Tourism** 82

READING SKILL: Understanding Connectors of Contrast 87

UNIT REVIEW 90

FIVE ANIMAL-HUMAN RELATIONSHIPS 92

READING 1   **Humans and Cattle: A Shared History** 94

READING SKILL: Inferring Meaning from the Text 100

READING 2   **Taming the Wild** 104

READING SKILL: Understanding Processes 109

UNIT REVIEW 112

SIX ARCHITECTURE 114

READING 1   **Safer Homes in Earthquake Zones** 116

READING SKILL: Understanding Information in Tables 122

READING 2   **Urban Architecture in the 21st Century** 126

READING SKILL: Taking Notes 132

UNIT REVIEW 136

GENETICS AND THE ENVIRONMENT   138

READING 1   **Sibling Personalities**   140

    READING SKILL: Analyzing Sentence
Purpose   144

READING 2   **Epigenetics**   148

    READING SKILL: Relating Supplementary
Material to the Text   154

UNIT REVIEW   158

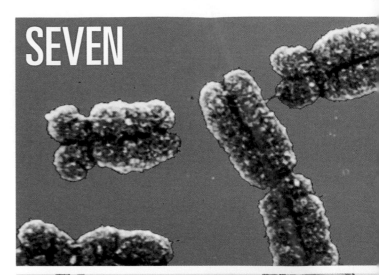

SEVEN

INVENTIONS   160

READING 1   **The Golden Age of Islamic Invention**   162

    READING SKILL: Scanning   167

READING 2   **Origami: The Practical Applications
of a Familiar Art**   172

    READING SKILL: Cohesion: Following
Topic Chains   177

UNIT REVIEW   182

EIGHT

ROBOTICS   184

READING 1   **Robots to the Rescue**   186

    READING SKILL: Reading as Test
Preparation   192

READING 2   **Humanoids**   196

    READING SKILL: Active Reading   201

UNIT REVIEW   206

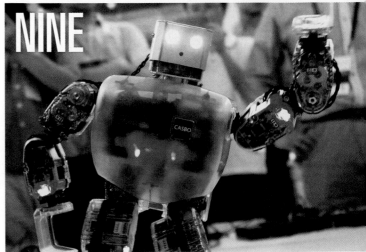

NINE

Vocabulary Index   208
Credits   211

INSIDE A UNIT

Architecture

FOCUS
1. How do the buildings you live and work in affect the way you live?
2. How do these buildings reflect the culture of the communities where they are located?

114   115

A laser show lights up Marina Bay, Singapore.

Each unit opens with an amazing **National Geographic** image that taps into learners' natural curiosity about the world while introducing the content that will be explored in the readings.

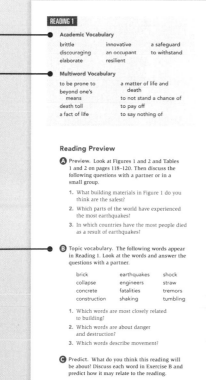

READING 1

Academic Vocabulary

brittle	innovative	a safeguard
discouraging	an occupant	to withstand
elaborate	resilient	

Multiword Vocabulary

to be prone to	a matter of life and death
beyond one's means	to not stand a chance of
death toll	to pay off
a fact of life	to say nothing of

Reading Preview

A Preview. Look at Figures 1 and 2 and Tables 1 and 2 on pages 118–120. Then discuss the following questions with a partner or in a small group.

1. What building materials in Figure 1 do you think are the safest?
2. Which parts of the world have experienced the most earthquakes?
3. In which countries have the most people died as a result of earthquakes?

B Topic vocabulary. The following words appear in Reading 1. Look at the words and answer the questions with a partner.

brick	earthquakes	shock
collapse	engineers	straw
concrete	fatalities	tremors
construction	shaking	tumbling

1. Which words are most closely related to building?
2. Which words are about danger and destruction?
3. Which words describe movement?

C Predict. What do you think this reading will be about? Discuss each word in Exercise B and predict how it may relate to the reading.

116   UNIT SIX Architecture

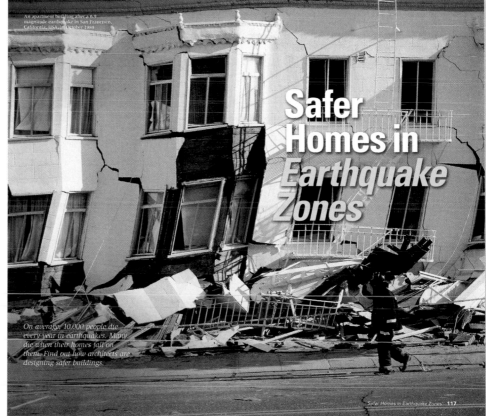

An apartment building after a 6.9 magnitude earthquake in San Francisco, California, USA, in October 1989.

Safer Homes in Earthquake Zones

On average, 10,000 people die every year in earthquakes. Many die when their homes fall on them. Find out how architects are designing safer buildings.

Safer Homes in Earthquake Zones   117

A comprehensive, three-part **vocabulary development program** builds student confidence as learners meet new or unfamiliar words in academic texts.

READING 1 SAFER HOMES IN EARTHQUAKE ZONES

One engineer sums it up in a few brief words: "Earthquakes don't kill; buildings do." In Los Angeles, Tokyo, and other wealthy cities in earthquake zones, high-tech, earthquake-resistant construction has become an expensive fact of life. Engineers reinforce concrete walls with steel. Some recent buildings rest on elaborate shock absorbers that have many layers of padding. Experts say these kinds of safeguards have paid off. They believe that strict building codes[1] saved thousands of lives when an earthquake hit Chile in 2010. It was the sixth most powerful earthquake on record. There was extensive damage. Yet, the death toll—521—was relatively low.

People in less developed countries have not been so lucky, however. Haiti also experienced a strong earthquake in 2010. Although the one in Chile was 500 times more powerful, the Haitian quake killed at least 223,000 people and left more than a million homeless (see Tables 1 and 2). In Haiti and other countries with few resources, expensive, earthquake-resistant structures don't stand a chance of getting built. Even basic earthquake engineering is often beyond their means. Billions of people live in houses that can't withstand the violent shaking of an earthquake. Fortunately, safer homes can be built cheaply, using local material such as straw, bamboo,[2] and recycled materials like old tires.

[1] building codes: government rules for safe construction

[2] bamboo: a tropical grass with hard, hollow stems

Table 1. Earthquakes with Highest Death Tolls since 1900

Country	Date	Magnitude	Fatalities
China	1976	7.0	242,000
Haiti	2010	7.0	223,000
China	1920	7.8	180,000
Indonesia	2004	9.1	165,000*
Japan	1923	7.9	143,000
Soviet Union (present day Turkmenistan)	1948	7.3	110,000
Italy	1908	7.1	75,000
Pakistan	2005	7.6	73,000
China	2008	7.9	69,000

*includes deaths from tsunami caused by earthquake
Source: EM-DAT, Centre for Research on the Epidemiology of Disasters

Table 2. Earthquakes with Highest Magnitudes since 1900

Country	Date	Magnitude	Fatalities
Chile	1960	9.5	1,655
Alaska, USA	1964	9.2	128
Indonesia	2004	9.1	165,000*
Japan	2011	9.0	16,000
Kamchatka, Soviet Union	1952	9.0	0
Chile	2010	8.8	521
off coast of Ecuador	1906	8.8	500–1,500
Alaska, USA	1965	8.7	0
Indonesia	2005	8.6	1,300

*includes deaths from tsunami caused by earthquake
Source: Australia Geographic

Figure 1. Inexpensive Earthquake-Resistant Construction

PAKISTAN

Light walls
Lightweight structures are subject to smaller forces and are less likely to fall when the ground shakes.

Quake-resistant houses are being built in Pakistan—of straw. The compressed bales are held together by nylon mesh and sandwiched between layers of plaster.

HAITI

Light roofs
In Haiti heavy concrete roofs collapsed on many homes; sheet metal roofs are more resilient.

Small windows
Small, regularly spaced openings create fewer weak spots in walls. But the bigger problem in Haiti was that walls were not properly reinforced.

PERU

Reinforced walls
The reinforcing rods need not be made of metal. Natural materials such as eucalyptus or bamboo work well too.

Bamboo

Mesh

In Peru the walls of some adobe houses have been fitted with a plastic mesh to prevent collapse.

INDONESIA

Shock absorbers
Tires filled with stones or sand and fastened between floor and foundation can serve as cheap shock absorbers for many types of building.

Source: National Geographic Magazine, June 2010

"The devastation in Haiti wouldn't happen in a developed country," says engineer Marcial Blondet of the Catholic University of Peru. Blondet has been working on innovative building ideas since 1970, when an earthquake in Peru killed 70,000 people. Many of the victims died when their houses crumbled around them. Heavy, brittle walls of traditional sundried brick cracked instantly when the ground started shaking. Subsequent tremors brought roofs tumbling down. Blondet's research team has found that brick walls like these can be reinforced with a strong plastic mesh.[3] In an earthquake, walls will crack, but they won't collapse. The occupants may lose their homes, but they won't lose their lives. This inexpensive plastic mesh can also reinforce concrete walls like the ones that are common in Haiti.

Engineers in other countries are also working on methods that use other types of inexpensive and local materials. Researchers in India have successfully tested concrete house walls reinforced with bamboo, which is both cheap and

[3] mesh: loosely woven material with big spaces, much like a net

Content-rich readings supported by real-world images, maps, charts, and informational graphics prepare learners for academic success.

After each reading . . .

READING COMPREHENSION

Big Picture

A Choose the best answer for each of the following questions.

1. What is the main idea of paragraph 1?
   a. Many countries cannot afford to build earthquake-resistant homes.
   b. The number of deaths from earthquakes is very high.
   c. Earthquake-resistant construction can save lives.

2. What is the purpose of paragraphs 3, 4, and 5?
   a. To show that engineers are helping communities that have experienced earthquakes
   b. To show that local and inexpensive building materials can be earthquake resistant
   c. To show the high-tech innovations in earthquake-resistant construction

3. The following sentence is the main idea for which paragraph?
   Although there are inexpensive ways to construct earthquake-resistant buildings, for some communities, these are still too expensive.
   a. Paragraph 4
   b. Paragraph 5
   c. Paragraph 6

4. What is the main idea of Reading 1?
   a. Earthquake-resistant construction is too expensive for some countries.
   b. Inexpensive earthquake-resistant construction is possible.
   c. More people will die in earthquakes if we don't build better houses.

B In Exercise A, question 2 suggests that paragraphs 3, 4, and 5 all have similar purposes. Write the main idea of each paragraph.

1. Paragraph 3: _____
2. Paragraph 4: _____
3. Paragraph 5: _____

Close-Up

A Briefly answer the following questions according to information in Reading 1.

1. Why was the earthquake damage so much worse in Haiti than in Chile?

2. How can plastic mesh help save lives?

3. What are the advantages of building materials such as bamboo and old tires?

4. Why is straw a good building material for areas that experience a lot of earthquakes?

Reading Comprehension sections assess learner comprehension through a variety of activities.

Learners are taught an essential **reading skill** and then apply that skill meaningfully to the reading.

Reading Skill

Understanding Information in Tables

Academic texts often include tables and graphs. These visuals may show information in the main text in a different form, or they may provide additional information. It is important to understand how the tables are connected to the main text.

1. Look for references to tables and graphs within the text (for example, *see Tables 1 and 2*). The surrounding text probably contains information closely connected to the information in the table.

2. Think about how the information in tables and graphs extends the ideas and arguments presented in the text.

A Look at Tables 1 and 2. Work with a partner to answer the following questions.

1. What information in the reading is also in the tables? Underline the overlapping information in the tables and the text.

2. For the events or ideas that you underlined in the reading, what additional information does the table provide?

B Compare the information in the two tables. Then discuss the following questions with a partner.

1. There were two earthquakes in the former Soviet Union only four years apart. Which earthquake had more fatalities? Why do you think the number of fatalities was so different?

2. Why do you think two of the most powerful earthquakes in the tables had no fatalities?

3. Which earthquake is listed in both Table 1 and Table 2? Why do you think only one earthquake is found in both tables?

4. What factors could explain the number of fatalities in both tables?

5. Based on the information in the tables, where do you think another major earthquake might occur in the future? Where do you think an earthquake with a high number of fatalities might occur? Explain your answers.

A FOCUS ON VOCABULARY

Academic Vocabulary sections develop the language that students are likely to encounter in authentic academic readings.

VOCABULARY PRACTICE

Academic Vocabulary

A Find the words in bold in Reading 1. Use the context and the sentences below to help you match each word to its correct definition.

_____ 1. The children spent days creating an **elaborate** (Par. 1) plan for a surprise birthday party.

_____ 2. The new law includes **safeguards** (Par. 1) against dangerous chemicals.

_____ 3. Airplane parts must **withstand** (Par. 2) the force of high winds and changes in temperature.

_____ 4. The engineers used **innovative** (Par. 3) methods to build the bridge.

_____ 5. Because their bones are **brittle** (Par. 3), it can be quite serious when old people fall.

_____ 6. All of the **occupants** (Par. 3) of the apartment building were able to escape the fire.

_____ 7. The plants in this area are naturally **resilient** (Par. 5) and grew back quickly after the drought.

_____ 8. The report was very **discouraging** (Par. 6). The police were unable to find the mountain climbers who got lost in the snowstorm.

a. stiff but easily broken

b. not easily harmed or damaged; able to recover

c. people who live inside a place

d. causing a feeling of hopelessness or lack of confidence to continue

e. new, different, and usually better

f. very complicated with many different parts

g. survive without damage

h. methods of protection from harm

B Choose an academic word from Exercise A to complete each of the following sentences. Notice and learn the words in bold because they often appear with the academic words.

1. In spite of the cold winter, the trees we planted last year turned out to be **remarkably** _____. This spring they are growing well.

2. In a special course, the teachers learned to use simple but _____ **ideas** in their classes to help students who struggle with their work.

3. The software engineers have created a(n) _____ **system** that no one understands. It is extremely complicated.

4. The _____ of the **building** say that the elevator needs repairs. Several people have gotten stuck in it.

5. The equipment is used in polar areas because it is able to _____ **extreme temperatures** and remain effective.

6. We were disappointed by the _____ **news** about the economy.

7. Older people often have _____ **bones** that break easily.

8. We must develop _____ **against** future natural disasters.

Safer Homes in Earthquake Zones **123**

Multiword Vocabulary sections identify words that are commonly grouped together and then prompt learners to work with them in different contexts for enhanced comprehension.

A collapsed building after the Haiti earthquake in 2010

Multiword Vocabulary

A Find the multiword vocabulary in bold in Reading 1 and use the context to help you figure out the meaning. Then match each item to the correct definition.

_____ 1. **a fact of life** (Par. 1)

_____ 2. **paid off** (Par. 1)

_____ 3. **death toll** (Par. 1)

_____ 4. **don't stand a chance of** (Par. 2)

_____ 5. **beyond their means** (Par. 2)

_____ 6. **a matter of life and death** (Par. 5)

_____ 7. **are prone to** (Par. 6)

_____ 8. **to say nothing of** (Par. 6)

a. the number of people who have died

b. have the tendency to be affected by something bad

c. extremely important; important enough to affect someone's survival

d. have no possibility of

e. in addition to and even more important than

f. was successful after a period of time

g. something that cannot be changed and must be accepted

h. too expensive for them

124 UNIT SIX *Architecture*

B Complete the following sentences using the correct multiword vocabulary from Exercise A. In some cases, you need to change the verb or pronoun form.

1. This has been a terrible winter. The temperatures have been extremely low, _____ the heavy snow.

2. The _____ from this weekend's tragic fire has reached four.

3. We would like to take a vacation this summer, but I am afraid, for now, it is _____. Maybe we will be able to afford it next year.

4. For top mountain climbers, having the right equipment can be _____. Poor preparations can have fatal consequences.

5. Our soccer team is not very strong this year. I am afraid we _____ making it to the championship match.

6. An investment in your education will _____ eventually because it will enable you to get a good job.

7. For people who live in Alaska, long, cold winters are just _____.

8. People who _____ respiratory problems should stay inside today. The pollution is very bad.

Use the Vocabulary

Write answers to the following questions. Use the words in bold in your answers. Then share your answers with a partner.

1. Are you **prone to** catching colds? If so, what are the best **safeguards against** catching them?

2. Some people believe that children are more **resilient** than adults following a serious illness or a tragedy. Do you think this is the case?

3. Have you ever made a plan or done something that others said **didn't stand a chance of** succeeding? Did your plan **pay off** in the end?

4. Most people dream of doing something or buying something that is **beyond their means**. What do you dream about?

5. What do you do when you get **discouraging news**? Do you accept it as **a fact of life**? Try to change it? Try to think about other things? Give an example of discouraging news you have heard.

In **Use the Vocabulary**, students get to activate the newly-learned vocabulary in new and interesting contexts.

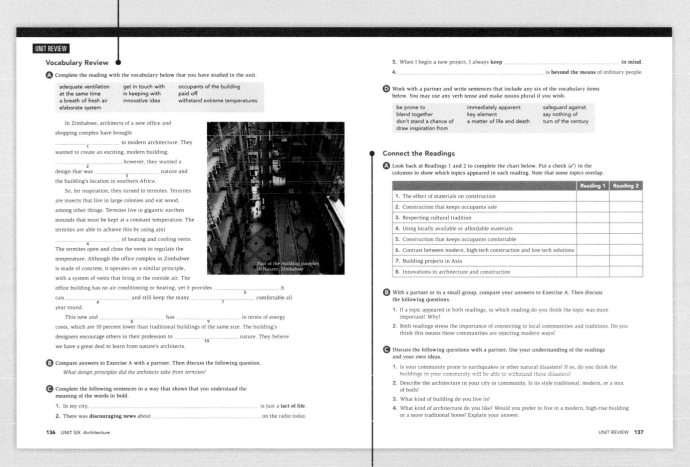

THINK AND DISCUSS

Work in a small group. Use the information in the reading and your own ideas to discuss the following questions.

1. **Summarize.** How would you describe the connection between the magnitude of an earthquake and the number of fatalities it causes?

2. **Analyze.** Reading 1 contains the following statement, "The occupants may lose their homes, but they won't lose their lives." Explain what this means. Should governments in these countries focus on expensive solutions, which may save buildings, or inexpensive solutions, which may not save the buildings themselves but will save the people inside these buildings?

3. **Predict.** How successful do you think the efforts to use inexpensive materials described in Reading 1 will be over time? Explain your answer.

Safer Homes in Earthquake Zones **125**

Think and Discuss questions at the end of each reading require learners to discuss their opinions on the topic while making connections to their own lives.

The **Vocabulary Review** recycles the key vocabulary from the unit and offers meaningful, contextualized practice opportunities.

UNIT REVIEW

Vocabulary Review

A Complete the reading with the vocabulary below that you have studied in the unit.

adequate ventilation	get in touch with	occupants of the building
at the same time	in keeping with	paid off
a breath of fresh air	innovative idea	withstand extreme temperatures
elaborate system		

In Zimbabwe, architects of a new office and shopping complex have brought _____ 1 _____ to modern architecture. They wanted to create an exciting, modern building. _____ 2 _____, however, they wanted a design that was _____ 3 _____ nature and the building's location in southern Africa.

So, for inspiration, they turned to termites. Termites are insects that live in large colonies and eat wood, among other things. Termites live in gigantic earthen mounds that must be kept at a constant temperature. The termites are able to achieve this by using a(n) _____ 4 _____ of heating and cooling vents. The termites open and close the vents to regulate the temperature. Although the office complex in Zimbabwe is made of concrete, it operates on a similar principle, with a system of vents that bring in the outside air. The office building has no air conditioning or heating, yet it provides _____ 5 _____. It can _____ 6 _____ and still keep the many _____ 7 _____ comfortable all year round.

This new and _____ 8 _____ has _____ 9 _____ in terms of energy costs, which are 10 percent lower than traditional buildings of the same size. The building's designers encourage others in their profession to _____ 10 _____ nature. They believe we have a great deal to learn from nature's architects.

B Compare answers to Exercise A with a partner. Then discuss the following question.

What design principles did the architects take from termites?

C Complete the following sentences in a way that shows that you understand the meaning of the words in bold.

1. In my city, _____ is just a **fact of life**.

2. There was **discouraging news** about _____ on the radio today.

3. When I begin a new project, I always **keep** _____ **in mind**.

4. _____ is **beyond the means** of ordinary people.

D Work with a partner and write sentences that include any six of the vocabulary items below. You may use any verb tense and make nouns plural if you wish.

be prone to	immediately apparent	safeguard against
blend together	key element	say nothing of
don't stand a chance of	a matter of life and death	turn of the century
draw inspiration from		

Connect the Readings

A Look back at Readings 1 and 2 to complete the chart below. Put a check (✓) in the columns to show which topics appeared in each reading. Note that some topics overlap.

	Reading 1	Reading 2
1. The effect of materials on construction		
2. Construction that keeps occupants safe		
3. Respecting cultural tradition		
4. Using locally available or affordable materials		
5. Construction that keeps occupants comfortable		
6. Contrast between modern, high-tech construction and low-tech solutions		
7. Building projects in Asia		
8. Innovations in architecture and construction		

B With a partner or in a small group, compare your answers to Exercise A. Then discuss the following questions.

1. If a topic appeared in both readings, in which reading do you think the topic was more important? Why?

2. Both readings stress the importance of connecting to local communities and traditions. Do you think this means these communities are rejecting modern ways?

C Discuss the following questions with a partner. Use your understanding of the readings and your own ideas.

1. Is your community prone to earthquakes or other natural disasters? If so, do you think the buildings in your community will be able to withstand these disasters?

2. Describe the architecture in your city or community. Is its style traditional, modern, or a mix of both?

3. What kind of building do you live in?

4. What kind of architecture do you like? Would you prefer to live in a modern, high-rise building or a more traditional home? Explain your answer.

136 UNIT SIX *Architecture*

UNIT REVIEW **137**

Caption on photo: *Part of the building complex in Harare, Zimbabwe*

Connect the Readings sections at the end of each unit practice critical thinking skills as learners are guided to compare, contrast, and synthesize information from the two readings.

SERIES INTRODUCTION

Welcome to National Geographic Learning's new Reading and Vocabulary Focus *series. The series delivers memorable reading experiences, develops essential reading skills, and showcases a wide variety of high-utility vocabulary. The passages take readers to exciting new places where they can apply the skills of successful academic readers. While engaged with the content, readers encounter target vocabulary that is ample, diverse, and presented with a fresh, pragmatic view of what the term vocabulary item truly means.*

Great reading classes depend on top-of-the-line content. That's why we've taken such great care in selecting content for *Reading and Vocabulary Focus*. Through all four levels (high beginning to low advanced), *Reading and Vocabulary Focus* draws from the vast resources of National Geographic. High-interest reading content written by some of the world's most authoritative and thought-provoking reporters and explorers is presented in level-appropriate language and used to build reading skills and to promote vocabulary learning. Skill building is of course important, but not for its own sake. Our goal is always, first and foremost, for students to enjoy working with readings that are truly interesting and worth reading.

A BROADBAND APPROACH TO VOCABULARY

A distinctive feature of *Focus* is its broadband approach to vocabulary. For each reading passage, three groups of vocabulary are called out:

1) 10–12 topic-related vocabulary items to consider in pre-reading activities
2) 6–8 academic words—single word items essential to building an academic vocabulary
3) 6–8 multiword vocabulary items useful in academic reading

A systematic focus on multiword vocabulary sets *Reading and Vocabulary Focus* apart from most reading/vocabulary texts. Increasingly, more and more teachers and many textbooks recognize that some vocabulary items consist of more than one word, especially phrasal/prepositional verbs (*hurry up, take on*) and compound nouns (*glass ceiling, weather station*). However, the amount of effort and text space devoted to expanding students' multiword repertoires is typically minimal and the approach haphazard.

Our thinking in the *Reading and Vocabulary Focus* series has been influenced by numerous researchers who have examined the great importance to native speakers of conventionalized multi-word units, whether those units are called "chunks," "strings," or something else. Schmitt and Carter settle on the term *formulaic sequences* and point out a helpful description by Wray, that formulaic sequences "are stored and retrieved whole from memory at the time of use rather than being subject to generation and analysis at the time of use by the language grammar." (Schmitt & Carter, 2012, 13)[1]

It is not always easy to decide whether a group of words constitutes a unit so tight and useful that it should be taught as a discrete vocabulary item. In our item selection for *Focus*, we applied the criterion of "stored and retrieved whole." An item could make the cut if, in the expert judgment of our authors and editors, it was probably treated cognitively as a whole thing. In this way, we were able to judge that such diverse language as *pay attention to, on the whole, an invasion of privacy*, and *be the first to admit* are formulaic sequences that learners should study and learn as whole units. We checked our judgment against as many sources as possible, including corpora such as the Bank of English (part of the Collins COBUILD corpus) and the online version of the *Corpus of Contemporary American English* (COCA).[2]

UNIT STRUCTURE

Each unit of *Reading and Vocabulary Focus* begins with a high-impact photograph related to the unit theme to capture the students' imaginations and allow for pre-reading discussion. The unit theme encourages inquiry and exploration and offers opportunities for synthesis of information. Two reading passages, related to each other thematically, form the heart of the unit. Each reading is followed by stages of comprehension work, reading skill practice, formative vocabulary exercises, and discussion. Finally the unit ends with a comprehensive vocabulary review section and critical thinking synthesizing tasks.

Pre-Reading and Reading

For each reading passage, pre-reading activities include a task that activates content schemata and a vocabulary exercise that provides a set of clues to the content that the reader will encounter while reading. Each reading has been chosen for high-interest and conceptual challenge and is presented in the company of some of the world's most stimulating photography and other graphics.

Comprehension and Vocabulary Development

Comprehension exercises after each reading start out with a focus on main ideas ("Big Picture") and move to details ("Close-Up"). Then a concise treatment of a high-utility reading skill leads into practice of the skill applied to the reading passage. The vocabulary section after each reading proceeds from the broadband approach mentioned earlier. First come exercises in recognizing

---

[1] Norbert Schmitt and Ronald Carter, Introduction to Formulaic Sequences: Acquisition, Processing, and Use, in Norbert Schmitt, ed. (2004), *Formulaic Sequences: Acquisition, Processing, and Use*, John Benjamins.

[2] At corpus.byu.edu/coca/

academic words and placing them in context. Many of the items in this section are from the Academic Word List (AWL); whether from the AWL or not, every "academic word" is important in academic discourse. Then comes a section of multiword vocabulary, focusing on formulaic sequences as described earlier in this introduction.

Discussion

After studying the vocabulary, students are prompted to use it in discussion activities. Finally, Think and Discuss questions at the end of each reading prompt learners to discuss their opinions on the topic of the reading while making connections to their own lives.

Unit Review

The *Unit Review* consists of two parts: Vocabulary Review and Connect the Readings. The first section of the vocabulary review draws together vocabulary of all types into a richly contextualized exercise. Learners then encounter and practice the vocabulary from the unit, strengthening semantic networks and integrating a wide variety of items into their repertoires. The second section of the unit review, Connect the Readings, takes students' critical-thinking skills to a very high level as they analyze both readings and discover similarities/differences, agreement/disagreement, and other concept relationships.

Reading and Vocabulary Focus has been conceived to respect the wide-ranging curiosity and critical-thinking power of contemporary students. Every day these readers encounter a flood of information. They face unprecedented demands to sort the significant from the trivial and to synthesize information. We are delighted to help them do this by offering great readings, engaging skills development, and top-tier vocabulary learning all in an inviting, visually striking form.

Lawrence J. Zwier
Series Consultant

THE
BODY
IN
MOTION

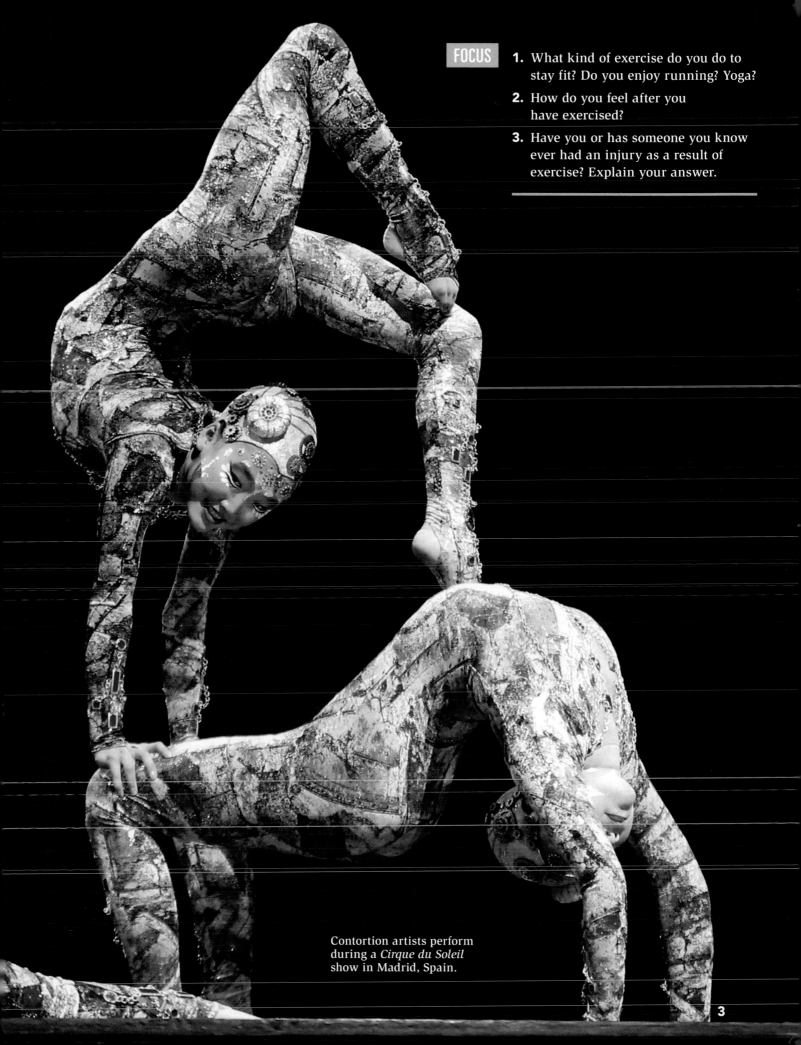

1. What kind of exercise do you do to stay fit? Do you enjoy running? Yoga?

2. How do you feel after you have exercised?

3. Have you or has someone you know ever had an injury as a result of exercise? Explain your answer.

Contortion artists perform during a *Cirque du Soleil* show in Madrid, Spain.

Academic Vocabulary

to collapse	impact	to trace
distinct	reinforced	to transfer
fundamental	terrain	

Multiword Vocabulary

to be known for	in the first place
to have an advantage over	not . . . at all
in an effort to	on the market
in shape	over the years

Reading Preview

A **Preview.** Look at the photos on pages 6–8 and read their captions. Then discuss the following questions with a partner or in a small group.

1. Does anything surprise you about how these runners are dressed? Explain your answer.

2. How are the shoes in the photos different?

3. How far do you think you could run in the Tarahumara shoes?

B **Topic vocabulary.** The following words appear in Reading 1. Look at the words and answer the questions with a partner.

absorb	distance	motion
arch	force	sole
athlete	heel	stride
barefoot	marathon	

1. Which words refer to parts of the foot?

2. Which words are related to running?

3. Which words are connected to movement and energy?

C **Predict.** What do you think this reading will be about? Discuss each word in Exercise B and predict how it may relate to the reading.

Millions of people around the world run for exercise. Do you know what kinds of shoes are best for running? You may be surprised by the answer.

A Natural Way to Run

A runner on a trail in the
Grand Canyon, Arizona, USA

Everyone knows that running is a good way   1
to stay in shape. The simplicity of running
appeals to many people. You don't need a
lot of complicated or expensive equipment; you
just need a good pair of running shoes. Well, that
idea is changing. Some researchers suggest that
perhaps you do not need shoes at all.

This is not a surprise to the Tarahumara   2
Indians, who live in northwestern Mexico. The
rough terrain in their area makes it easier to travel
on foot than by horse or by car. Traditionally,
the Tarahumara were hunters. They followed
their prey[1] over long distances, sometimes for
days, until the animals became exhausted and

---

[1] *prey:* animals that are hunted

Tarahumarans running in simple rubber-soled shoes

Scientific studies are beginning to point to something the Tarahumara have known for centuries: Human beings are built for running barefoot. In a recent study, researchers used a video camera to examine how athletes run when they are barefoot. The study revealed that barefoot runners land on the middle of their foot. When they do this, the arch of the foot absorbs the impact. Then that force is redirected back up through the leg.

As we look at the side view of a barefoot 5 runner, we can begin to understand why this makes sense. The natural, barefoot stride has two distinct advantages over running in shoes. First, the raised arch is the foot's natural shock absorber.[2] As the force of impact drives the foot toward the ground, the arch flattens and expands. It absorbs the energy of impact. Second, as the foot leaves the ground, that energy travels back up the leg. This helps the leg move upward into the next step. One way to understand this is to imagine the arch as a trampoline: The downward motion is redirected into an upward force, increasing the runner's speed and efficiency (see Figure 1).

---

[2] *shock absorber:* a piece of equipment, usually on a car, that makes it more comfortable to travel over a bumpy surface

collapsed. As a result, for the Tarahumara, running very long distances became part of daily life. They are known for their endurance, running races of 50 miles (80 kilometers) or longer. When Tarahumara athletes ran in the marathon at the 1968 Olympics, they did not understand that the race was over after only 26.2 miles, so they kept running. "Too short. Too short," they complained.

But here is the amazing part: Tarahumara 3 runners don't wear running shoes. Tarahumara shoes are very simple. The sole is a piece of rubber held to the foot with homemade straps. These rubber soles protect against sharp objects, but they don't provide any support or cushioning.

How is it possible that some of the best 4 runners in the world don't wear running shoes?

Figure 1. Downward Motion Leads to Upward Force

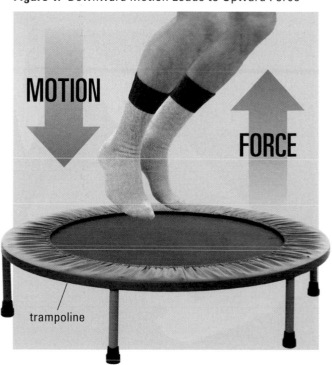

MOTION

FORCE

trampoline

Figure 2. Comparison of Two Running Strides

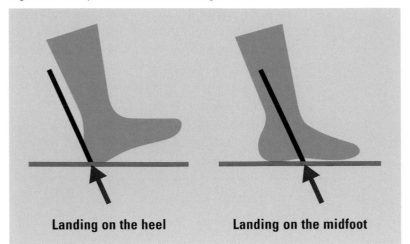

Landing on the heel Landing on the midfoot

The researchers also analyzed running with shoes. The study showed that runners in shoes usually land on their heels instead of the middle of their feet (see Figure 2). This creates two problems. First, the force of impact is not transferred into the upward leg as part of the motion of running. In fact, the heel acts like a brake, which slows the runner down. The second, more serious problem is that most of the energy is absorbed by the heel, which is not designed to handle this force. Various running injuries to the knee, calf, and foot can be traced to this repeated impact.

6

In an effort to prevent these common injuries, over the years shoe companies have designed special running shoes to reduce the impact of running and protect the heel. Many of these shoes have higher heels that are reinforced with air pockets, gel, or dense material that absorbs the impact to the heel. Unfortunately, recent research suggests that these shoes also encourage runners to land on their heels, which is what causes injuries in the first place.

7

In response to this more recent research, shoe companies have started to reconsider the fundamental design of running shoes. Walk into a sporting goods store today, and you will find sections that are devoted to "minimalist"[3] shoes. With a thin sole and heel, they are designed to encourage a runner's natural stride. In other words, they are shoes that feel like no shoes. The increasing number of these shoes on the market is evidence of this new trend. It is clear that shoe companies and runners are beginning to accept the wisdom of the Tarahumara—barefoot may be best.

8

---

[3] *minimalist:* using the simplest form or structure

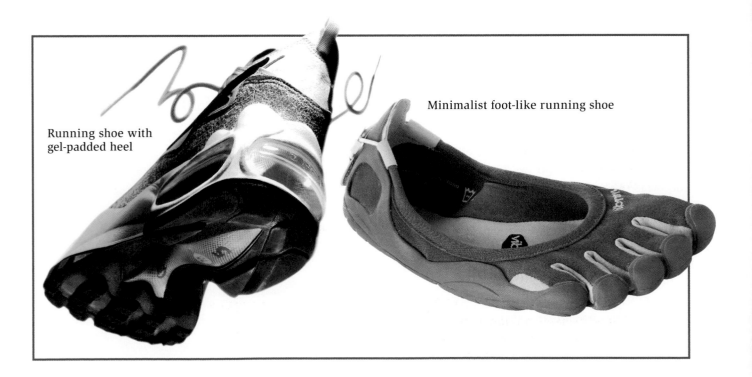

Running shoe with gel-padded heel

Minimalist foot-like running shoe

READING COMPREHENSION

Big Picture

A Read the following statements. Check (✓) the four statements that express the main ideas of Reading 1.

_____ **1.** Some of the world's best endurance runners do not wear running shoes.

_____ **2.** Landing on your heels can slow you down and cause injury.

_____ **3.** The arch is the foot's natural shock absorber.

_____ **4.** Shoe companies need to keep up with the latest research on running.

_____ **5.** Running barefoot—or almost barefoot—is better for your body.

_____ **6.** Higher heels are not the best solution to running injuries.

_____ **7.** A natural stride—that is, landing on the middle of the foot—is faster and healthier.

_____ **8.** Tarahumara athletes use a piece of rubber with straps as shoes.

B Which statement in Exercise A best expresses the main idea of the *whole* reading?

Close-Up

A Choose the best answer for each of the following questions. In some cases, two answers are correct.

1. How did the Tarahumara hunt animals?
   a. They shot them from a great distance.
   b. They ran after them for a long distance.
   c. They waited for them to get tired.

2. What is the purpose of the Tarahumara's shoes?
   a. Protection from impact
   b. Cultural expression
   c. Protection from rocks or other sharp things

3. How long was the race that Tarahumara athletes ran in 1968?
   a. 26.2 miles
   b. 50 miles
   c. Hundreds of miles

4. What part of a barefoot runner's foot hits the ground first?
   a. The heel
   b. The middle of the foot
   c. The toes

5. Why is running barefoot superior to running in shoes?
   a. It allows the foot and leg to absorb the impact.
   b. It is more efficient.
   c. It uses more energy.

6. According to paragraph 5 and Figure 1, how is jumping on a trampoline similar to running?
   a. It is the same motion as running.
   b. Athletes enjoy both activities.
   c. Both actions change a downward force into an upward force.

7. What is the effect of landing on your heel?
   a. It slows you down.
   b. It transfers the impact.
   c. It absorbs all of the impact in one small place.

8. According to the reading, what causes most running injuries?
   a. Sharp objects
   b. Repeated impact
   c. Badly designed shoes

9. What is the effect of using running shoes with reinforced heels?
   a. They protect runners' heels from impact.
   b. They encourage runners to land on their heels.
   c. They improve runners' stride.

10. What name would you choose if you wanted to sell minimalist shoes?
   a. High-Impact Shoes
   b. Barefoot Shoes
   c. Gel Shoes

B Compare answers to Exercise A with a partner. Explain your answers.

Reading Skill

Connecting Visual Materials to a Text

Understanding illustrations, photos, maps, and other visual materials can help deepen your understanding of a text. It is useful to "read" these visual materials before you read the text. Then, as you read the text, look for connections to the visuals. See how the visual materials explain or illustrate concepts in the text. Taking time to look closely at visual materials will improve your comprehension.

A Answer the following questions about the photos and illustrations in Reading 1. Give the paragraph numbers.

1. Look at the photo at the bottom of page 6. What paragraph does it help you understand? _____

2. Look at the photo of the shoes at the bottom of page 8. What paragraphs does it help you understand? _____

3. What paragraph does Figure 1 help you understand? _____

4. What paragraph does Figure 2 help you understand? _____

B Compare answers to Exercise A with a partner. Then discuss the following questions.

1. Which visual materials helped you the most in understanding the reading?

2. Would you be able to understand the reading without them?

3. If you could add one more photo or illustration to help you understand the reading, what would it be?

VOCABULARY PRACTICE

Academic Vocabulary

A Find the words in bold in Reading 1. Use the paragraph numbers to help you. Then use the context to help you match each word to its correct definition.

_____ 1. **terrain** (Par. 2)   **a.** basic and centrally important

_____ 2. **collapsed** (Par. 2)   **b.** made stronger

_____ 3. **impact** (Par. 4)   **c.** moved from one place to another

_____ 4. **distinct** (Par. 5)   **d.** force

_____ 5. **transferred** (Par. 6)   **e.** fell down suddenly

_____ 6. **traced** (Par. 6)   **f.** kind of land

_____ 7. **reinforced** (Par. 7)   **g.** connected back to

_____ 8. **fundamental** (Par. 8)   **h.** clear and easy to notice

B Choose an academic word from Exercise A to complete each of the following sentences.

1. The _____ of the falling tree broke the window.

2. She _____ her family history all the way to its origins in Ethiopia.

3. Although there is no signature, the style of the painting is quite _____. Experts are certain that it is the work of Picasso.

4. The buildings did not fall in the earthquake because their walls were _____ with steel.

5. The first and most _____ principle of medicine is not to hurt patients.

6. Last month he _____ his savings and checking accounts to a new bank.

7. A major storm hit the town and many of the older buildings _____.

8. Some cars can be driven on all different kinds of _____, from rocky mountains to sandy beaches.

C The words in bold show academic words from Exercise A and words they often appear with. Complete the sentences with your own ideas.

1. He decided to **transfer** his **money** _____.

2. You can **trace** the **history** of _____ to _____.

3. _____ through **rough** mountain **terrain**.

4. _____ was **reinforced with** extra wires.

5. _____ the **impact** of the **crash**.

6. There is a **fundamental difference** between _____ and _____.

7. _____ several **distinct characteristics**.

8. _____ **collapsed under** the weight of the snow.

Multiword Vocabulary

A Find the multiword vocabulary in bold in Reading 1. Use the paragraph numbers to help you. Then use the context to help you figure out the meaning and match each item to the correct definition.

_____ 1. **in shape** (Par. 1)   **a.** for sale

_____ 2. **not . . . at all** (Par. 1)   **b.** in good health or condition

_____ 3. **are known for** (Par. 2)   **c.** in order to try to

_____ 4. **has** two distinct **advantages over** (Par. 5)   **d.** in the beginning, in the original situation

_____ 5. **in an effort to** (Par. 7)   **e.** is better in some specific ways

_____ 6. **over the years** (Par. 7)   **f.** over a period of time

_____ 7. **in the first place** (Par. 7)   **g.** are familiar to many people because of

_____ 8. **on the market** (Par. 8)   **h.** not in any way or any form

B Complete the following sentences with the correct multiword vocabulary from Exercise A. In some cases, you need to change the word form.

1. Running _____ exercising in a gym. It's cheaper and doesn't require equipment.

2. _____, she has begun to look more and more like her mother.

3. The house has been _____ for two years, and it hasn't sold yet.

4. There was over a foot of snow in January, but in February, it did _____ snow _____.

5. Belize and the Bahamas _____ for their beautiful beaches and spectacular diving.

6. _____ reduce pollution, Mexico City does not permit drivers to use their cars one day every week.

7. It's no surprise that the mayor is in jail. I never trusted him _____.

8. There are many different ways to stay _____. Some people swim, others play tennis, and some people like to dance.

Use the Vocabulary

Write answers to the following questions. Use the words in bold in your answers. Then share your answers with a partner.

1. Many people, especially children and teenagers, do not get enough exercise. How can society **reinforce** good habits such as walking instead of driving, and reducing sugar and fat in our diets?

2. What do you do to stay **in shape**? Has your exercise routine changed **over the years**?

3. Do you think some forms of exercise **have an advantage over** others in helping you stay fit? Explain your opinion.

4. Health experts say that too many people in developed countries are getting fat. **In an effort to** address this problem, many schools do not allow children to buy candy or unhealthy snacks and drinks. Do you agree with this policy?

5. Do you watch sports? Do you think sports such as soccer and baseball have a **fundamental** value? What kind of **impact** do they have on society? Explain your opinion.

6. What sports **is** your country or city best **known for**?

THINK AND DISCUSS

Work in a small group. Use the information in the reading and your own ideas to discuss the following questions.

1. **Summarize.** How have the Tarahumara become such incredible long-distance runners?

2. **Apply knowledge.** One running expert suggests this experiment: *Find an old video of a runner when he or she was a young child running around. It is likely that the child has a natural stride. Then watch the runner as an adult. It is likely that the runner has lost the natural stride.* Why do you think runners often lose the ability to run naturally, as they did when they were children?

3. **Apply knowledge.** Try running for a short distance. Which part of your foot do you land on? On your heel or the middle of your foot? Then try to change your stride and the part of your foot you land on. How easily could you change the way you run?

4. **Predict.** Do you think minimalist shoes are just a fashion that will soon pass? Or, do you think they will become a common running shoe? Explain your answer.

Academic Vocabulary

to confirm	optimal	stability
intense	persistent	a strategy
motivation	a sensation	

Multiword Vocabulary

to be the case	in a good mood
to conduct a study	in this way
an extended period of time	to play a role in
to have an edge over	positive feedback

You feel tired but good after exercising. Why does your body respond in this way? Find out how this response may be related to our distant past, when humans hunted animals on foot.

Reading Preview

A **Preview.** Scan Reading 2 and Table 1 on page 16 to find answers to the following questions.

1. What is a runner's high?

2. How fast can humans run?

3. Who is Dr. Raichlen?

B **Topic vocabulary.** The following words appear in Reading 2. Look at the words and answer the questions with a partner.

advantage	exercise	prey
ancestor	exhausted	speed
boost	hunting	survival
endurance	mammals	sweat

1. Which words are related to early humans?

2. Which words are related to running?

3. Which words are positive in meaning?

C **Predict.** What do you think this reading will be about? Discuss each word in Exercise B and predict how it may relate to the reading.

A young man jumps across a path in the Golden Canyon, California, USA.

THE
RUNNER'S
HIGH

THE RUNNER'S HIGH

Running fast, swimming far, biking hard. All of these are examples of intense physical exercise. Intense exercise for a long period of time may give you a sensation known as a "runner's high." This is a feeling of extreme happiness, or euphoria. After intense physical activity, the brain responds by releasing certain chemicals that increase your energy and put you in a good mood. 1

Why do humans have such a response? Did it give humans some advantage in the past? Scientists think this may be the case. They believe that this response to exercise may have helped early humans to survive. Survival depended on hunting successfully and escaping enemies. Both required a lot of running. However, human beings are not very fast, compared to many other mammals. For example, the cheetah can reach speeds of up to 70 miles per hour (about 112 kilometers per hour). Even bears can get up to about 35 mph (56 kph). Fast human runners can only manage around 20 mph (32 kph), and they can only run this fast for a short distance. Although we are slower than many other mammals (see Table 1), we do have an edge over them. 2

Our edge is endurance. We may not be fast, but our bodies are designed to run for an extended period of time. Our long legs use energy efficiently, and our broad shoulders help maintain balance and stability over long distances. Millions of sweat glands[1] and lack of fur help keep the body cool during vigorous exercise. Endurance would have been very important to our ancestors because they could not outrun the animals that they hunted. Instead, early hunters were persistent. Their strategy was to separate one animal from a herd. Then they would follow the animal until it collapsed from exhaustion. In this way, they were able to hunt animals that were bigger, stronger, and faster. Scientists believe the runner's high very likely gave early humans the necessary energy and motivation during long hunts. Even when they 3

Cheetahs can reach speeds of 70 mph.

Brown bear

were exhausted, this kept them going until they captured their prey.

David Raichlen, an anthropology professor at the University of Arizona, conducted a study of mammals for whom running was once a survival strategy. He wanted to confirm that this response—the runner's high—is characteristic of such mammals. He compared running mammals such as humans and dogs with mammals that don't need to run for long periods in order to survive. For the second group, he chose ferrets, which sleep up to 21 hours a day and run only 4

____

[1] *sweat glands:* small organs in the skin that produce perspiration. They help cool the body.

Table 1. Maximum Speeds of Animals

Animal	Maximum Speed (mph)	Animal	Maximum Speed (mph)
Cheetah	70	Bear	35
Lion	50	Cat	30
Horse	50	Elephant	25
Dog	45	Human	20
Zebra	40	Mouse	8

Source: Texas Parks and Wildlife/Factmonster

Ferret

for brief periods. After 30 minutes of exercise, the humans and dogs showed an increase in the brain chemicals that create the runner's high. The ferrets' brains showed no such change. Raichlen concluded that humans and dogs are not only born to run, they are also hardwired[2] to like it. They get positive feedback in the form of pleasure from intense and prolonged exercise.

It is true that the runner's high no longer 5 plays a role in modern hunting. However, it may help modern humans to stay in shape. With extended exercise, there is a boost in mood and energy, which may motivate people to continue exercising. Prolonged exercise improves the condition of the heart and lungs and helps maintain an optimal weight—characteristics of long, healthy lives. The runner's high helped our ancestors to survive; it may just do the same for us today.

_____

[2] *hardwired:* designed to automatically behave in a certain way

READING COMPREHENSION

Big Picture

Ⓐ The following statements are the main ideas of each paragraph in Reading 2. Write the correct paragraph number next to its main idea. One of the statements is *not* a main idea from the reading. Write an *X* next to this statement.

_____ 1. The brain's response to running probably helped early humans to survive.

_____ 2. For early humans, endurance was important for successful hunting.

_____ 3. The brain's response to exercise can be as helpful today as it was in the past.

_____ 4. Running is an important strategy for all mammals.

_____ 5. Intense exercise can make you feel good.

_____ 6. A study showed that with both dogs and humans, the brain's response to exercise is pleasure.

Ⓑ Read the following statements. Check (✓) the statement that best expresses the main idea of the *whole* reading.

_____ 1. Endurance helped early humans to survive by improving their hunting.

_____ 2. Human beings have always enjoyed running, and they still do today.

_____ 3. Long-distance running helped early humans survive, and it continues to be a beneficial activity today.

_____ 4. The human body has adapted an ability to run for long distances.

Close-Up

A Decide which of the following statements are true or false according to the reading. Write *T* (True) or *F* (False) next to each one.

_____ 1. A walk in the park is likely to result in a runner's high.

_____ 2. The brain's response to running is a recent change in human development.

_____ 3. Bears can run almost twice as fast as humans.

_____ 4. Humans can run at high speeds.

_____ 5. Running for long distances was an important survival strategy for early humans.

_____ 6. Early humans were only able to hunt smaller, slower animals.

_____ 7. The runner's high contributes to endurance.

_____ 8. Like humans, ferrets have had to run to survive.

_____ 9. Dogs also get a runner's high.

_____ 10. The runner's high no longer has a function in our lives.

B Work with a partner or in a small group. Change the false statements in Exercise A to make them true.

Reading Skill

Connecting Ideas with Signal Words: *this*, *these*, and *such*

In texts, you will notice adjectives, adverbs, and pronouns such as *this*, *these*, and *such* often connect ideas across sentences. These words refer to ideas that appear earlier in the text.

- *This* and *these* may refer to either a noun phrase or a longer piece of text that expresses an entire idea or concept.

  *Health professionals recommend that everyone should get **30 minutes of exercise a day**. This is easy to accomplish by walking or biking to work or school.*

- *Such* also refers to noun phrases that appear earlier in the text, but it has the meaning of *like that/those*. In the example below, *such suggestions* means *suggestions like those*.

  *Health professionals have also suggested that **adults reduce the amount of salt and fat in their diets**. Unfortunately, such suggestions are often ignored.*

A Find and underline the instances of the signal words *this* (7), *these* (1), and *such* (3) in the reading.

B Read the sentences that precede the signal words you underlined in Exercise A. For each signal word, find the word, phrase, or idea that it refers to. Fill in the chart below. The first one is done for you.

Signal Word	What does the signal word refer to?
1. these (Par. 1)	*running fast, swimming far, biking hard*
2. this (Par. 1)	
3. such a (Par. 2)	
4. this (Par. 2)	
5. this (Par. 2)	
6. this (Par. 2)	
7. this (Par. 3)	
8. this (Par. 3)	
9. this (Par. 4)	
10. such (Par. 4)	
11. such (Par. 4)	

VOCABULARY PRACTICE

Academic Vocabulary

A Read the following sentences from Reading 2. Use the context of each word in bold to match it to its correct definition. Write the correct letter on the line before each sentence.

_____ 1. Running fast, swimming far, biking hard. All of these are examples of **intense** physical exercise.

_____ 2. Intense exercise for a long period of time may give you a **sensation** known as a "runner's high."

_____ 3. Our long legs use energy efficiently, and our broad shoulders help maintain balance and **stability** over long distances.

_____ 4. Instead, early hunters were **persistent**. Their strategy was to separate one animal from a herd. Then they would follow the animal until it collapsed from exhaustion.

_____ 5. Their **strategy** was to separate one animal from a herd.

_____ 6. Scientists believe the runner's high very likely gave early humans the necessary energy and **motivation** to persist during long hunts.

_____ 7. He wanted to **confirm** that this neurological response is characteristic of such mammals.

_____ 8. Prolonged exercise improves the condition of the heart and lungs and helps maintain an **optimal** weight—characteristics of long, healthy lives.

a. feeling

b. to show that an idea or belief is a fact

c. the desire to do something

d. serious; extreme

e. the state of being fixed; unlikely to move or fall

f. continuing to do something past the expected time

g. ideal; the best

h. planned actions for achieving a goal

B Choose an academic word from Exercise A to complete each of the following sentences. Notice and learn the words in bold because they often appear with the academic words.

1. Everyone was excited because the snowstorm created _____ **conditions** for skiing.

2. The company is very successful because it has developed an **effective** _____ for attracting new customers.

3. There was _____ **pressure** during the week before the exam, but fortunately it did not last long.

4. Before you act, you should _____ your **suspicions**. It is always better to be sure.

5. You need to find a way to resolve this _____ **problem**. It has been going on for too long.

6. True leaders often find the _____ **to continue** even when the situation looks hopeless.

7. The 1980s were a time of **political** _____. There were not many significant changes or problems during that period.

8. She felt a **strange** _____ in her stomach as the plane left the ground.

Multiword Vocabulary

A Find the words in bold in Reading 2, using the paragraph numbers given. Then use the words from the box below to complete the multiword vocabulary.

an edge over	mood	role in	the case
feedback	period of time	study	this way

1. **in a good** _____ (Par. 1)

2. **be** _____ (Par. 2)

3. **have** _____ (Par. 2)

4. **an extended** _____ (Par. 3)

5. **in** _____ (Par. 3)

6. **conducted a** _____ (Par. 4)

7. **positive** _____ (Par. 4)

8. **plays a** _____ (Par. 5)

B Choose the correct definition for the multiword vocabulary in bold.

1. Exercise **plays an** important **role in** good heart health.
   a. leads to   **b.** is a factor in

2. Scientists used to believe that the brain was inactive during sleep, but now they know that this **is not the case**.
   a. is not true   **b.** is not possible

3. Students who receive **positive feedback** such as good grades and praise from their teacher and parents often do better in school.
   a. responses that encourage them to   **b.** reasons to do something that they don't
        keep doing something   like to do

4. Most newspapers now have online editions. **In this way**, they have been able to increase the number of readers.
   a. like this   **b.** in the future

5. Scientists **conducted a study** to determine the effect of the new drug.

  a. asked patients   **b.** did an experiment

6. Astronauts stayed on the space station for **an extended period of time**.

  a. a short time   **b.** a long time

7. She is **in a good mood** because she is going on vacation tomorrow.

  a. feeling happy   **b.** feeling energetic

8. He speaks three languages, so he **has an edge over** the other applicants for the position.

  a. is more advanced than   **b.** has an advantage compared to

Use the Vocabulary

Write answers to the following questions. Use the words in bold in your answers. Then share your answers with a partner.

1. What kinds of activities put you **in a good mood**?

2. What do you do when you are in a bad mood for **an extended period of time**?

3. Do you think diet and exercise **play a role in** your moods? Explain.

4. Think of several tasks that are difficult for you. Are you usually **persistent** in these tasks, or do you give up easily? How do you find the **motivation** to continue?

5. What are the **optimal conditions** that keep you working when you are studying something that does not interest you?

6. Some experts believe that **positive feedback** is essential for maintaining high performance in sports. Do you think this **is the case**? Why, or why not?

THINK AND DISCUSS

Work in a small group. Use the information in the reading and your own ideas to discuss the following questions.

1. Evaluate. The reading claims that endurance was important for early human hunters. What archaeological evidence do you think there is for this?

2. Use prior knowledge. What other strategies do you think early humans had that helped them to survive?

3. Make connections. In what ways do you think these strategies are still productive for modern humans?

4. Analyze. Are there any ways in which these strategies are counterproductive? In other words, is it possible that they may be harmful to modern humans?

5. Give opinions. The study suggests that dogs get pleasure from running. Do you think this is true? Give reasons for your answer.

Vocabulary Review

(A) Complete the reading with the vocabulary below that you have studied in the unit.

are known for	optimal conditions
an extended period of time	over the years
have an edge over	play a role
in shape	positive feedback
motivation to continue	rough terrain

If you have ever run or watched a marathon, you know it requires considerable endurance to run 26.2 miles. Some runners give up before the end, but others find the _____ 1 running. What can explain this difference? Runners from some parts of the world seem to be especially good at marathons. For example, athletes who live and train at high altitudes generally _____ 2 other athletes in long-distance races. Their hearts use oxygen more efficiently, so they can run for _____ 3 without getting tired or out of breath.

Kenya and Ethiopia _____ 4 their long-distance runners. _____ 5, some of the best marathoners in these two nations have come from mountainous regions with _____ 6. It seems that these are _____ 7 for an athlete to build strength and get _____ 8. Yet, this cannot be the only explanation for the success of these athletes. Not all mountainous regions produce long-distance runners. Another reason may be that most of these runners have light, thin bodies. Experts believe that this may _____ 9 in their success in marathons. A final factor may be that they get _____ 10 from running. Not only do they get financial rewards, but success can lead to national popularity in Kenya and Ethiopia.

(B) Compare answers to Exercise A with a partner. Then discuss the following question.

Which factor do you think is the most important for a runner's success?

C Complete the following sentences in a way that shows that you understand the meaning of the words in bold.

1. I am **in a good mood** today because _____.

2. There is a **fundamental difference** between _____.

3. Scientists **conducted a study** to find _____.

4. _____ is a **persistent problem** in _____.

D Work with a partner and write sentences that include any six of the vocabulary items below. You may use any verb tense and make nouns plural if you wish.

be the case	effective strategy	in the first place	on the market
confirm a suspicion	have an advantage over	intense pressure	strange sensation
distinct characteristic	in an effort to		

Connect the Readings

A Review Readings 1 and 2. In what way is the human body uniquely adapted for running long distances? Make a list of these characteristics.

_____

_____

_____

B With a partner or in a small group, compare answers to Exercise A. Then fill out the chart below with information about the scientific studies in the readings. The answers may not be stated directly in the readings. You may have to draw your own conclusions about them.

	Reading 1	Reading 2
1. What question(s) were the researchers trying to answer?		
2. Who were the subjects in the study?		
3. What did the subjects do in the study?		
4. What did the researchers find out?		

C Discuss the following questions with a partner. Use your understanding of the readings and your own ideas.

1. Although many experts believe that running barefoot or with minimalist shoes is better for us, why do most runners wear running shoes with lots of support and material that absorbs impact?

2. Humans are uniquely suited to sustained and intense exercise, which can be a source of pleasure for humans and some other mammals. If this is true, why do so few people, especially in developed countries, engage in intensive exercise?

FOCUS

1. How is the length of the day related to the movement of the Earth and sun?

2. How is the length of the year related to the movement of the Earth and sun?

3. Do all cultures measure time in the same way? Explain your answer.

TIME

A photo taken over many hours in the Carpathian Mountains, eastern Europe, shows the movement of the stars as the Earth moves through time and space.

Academic Vocabulary

to conserve	equivalent	to promote
consumption	a justification	valid
to contradict	mandatory	

Multiword Vocabulary

all year round	to follow suit
to be at a higher risk of	to make a proposal
to be worth the trouble	no matter what
to commit a crime	on a national scale

Reading Preview

A **Preview.** Look at the photos and map on pages 28–30 of the reading. Then discuss the following questions with a partner or in a small group.

1. What does *DST* mean?

2. What do you know about DST?

3. Does your country observe DST?

B **Topic vocabulary.** The following words appear in Reading 1. Look at the words and answer the questions with a partner.

adjust	coal	generate
adopt	curtains	sunrise
air-conditioning	electricity	sunset
candles		

1. Which words relate to light?

2. Which words might be used to talk about energy?

3. Which words describe change?

C **Predict.** What do you think this reading will be about? Discuss each word in Exercise B and predict how it may relate to the reading.

Why do people in some countries set their clocks forward and back during the year? Read about the history of efforts to make time work for us.

A man sets a large clock back an hour in Minsk, Belarus, to signify the end of daylight saving time.

Spring
Forward,
Fall
Back

SPRING FORWARD, FALL BACK

One morning every spring, people all over 1 Europe, North America, and other parts of the world stagger out of bed and drag themselves to work or school. Some arrive late; others arrive sleepy. Then, one morning the next fall, they wake up, look gratefully at their clocks, and go back to sleep for another hour.

The reason? Every spring, these people move 2 their clocks forward one hour when daylight saving time (DST) begins. They move them back one hour in the fall when it ends. It seems like a lot of trouble. Why do we do have DST in the first place? For answers, we have to go back several hundred years.

How Did It All Start?

One summer morning in Paris in 1784, the 3 American inventor and diplomat Benjamin Franklin woke up at six in the morning. Usually, he stayed out very late and so, on most days, he slept until about noon. Like many people then and now, his activities were controlled by the clock, not the light of the sun. That day, however, he had forgotten to close the curtains so his room became very bright early in the morning. He was delighted that he had six extra hours of daylight that day, which would cost him nothing. In contrast, his evening activities required expensive, smoky candles. When he realized

A notice informs the British public to move their clocks back one hour in September 1916.

this, he calculated how much the people of Paris could save on candles if they all got out of bed at sunrise during the summer. He came up with a figure that is equivalent to $200 million today. These calculations led him to make a proposal to use daylight more efficiently by changing the clocks twice a year.

For a long time, however, DST remained 4 only a proposal. The first country to adopt it on a national scale was Germany in 1916 during World War I. By then, coal was used to generate electricity, and the German government wanted to save the coal for the military. Other countries on both sides of the war quickly followed suit. During World War II, DST became mandatory all year round in Britain and the United States. (See Figure 1 on page 30 for other countries that have adopted DST.) As in World War I, governments wanted to conserve energy for the war effort. Thirty years later, the United States again extended DST throughout the year during the 1973–74 oil crisis.[1]

Why Do We Do It Today?

Since DST was first proposed, the major jus- 5 tification for DST has been energy conservation. But does setting our clocks forward an hour in the spring really still save energy? Maybe. A 2008

---

[1] *1973–74 oil crisis:* a world shortage of oil that occurred when oil-producing countries stopped shipping oil to some western countries and reduced production

U.S. government study showed that DST reduced the country's energy consumption by 0.02 percent. Although the percentage seems small, the savings can add up because the United States consumes so much energy.

However, several other studies contradict 6 these findings. A team of environmental economists found that in Australia, DST reduced energy consumption in the evening because sunset was later. But with sunrise also coming later, DST resulted in higher electricity use during the dark mornings. A study in the United States found that although use of lights decreased as a result of DST, the use of air-conditioning rose because the extra hour in the summer evening is hotter.

So, Why Do We Still Do It?

If the impact on energy conservation is 7 uncertain, why do so many countries continue to observe DST? Supporters of DST offer three additional arguments: The extra hour of light in the evening can boost business. People continue to shop and engage in outdoor activities until later in the evening, which is beneficial for the economy. Second, supporters claim that the time change can promote safety by reducing both crime and traffic accidents. People are more likely to commit crimes and drive in the evening than the early morning. However, the strongest claim for the benefits of DST is that it can promote a healthier lifestyle by encouraging people to be more active in the evening.

Figure 1. Daylight Saving Time around the World

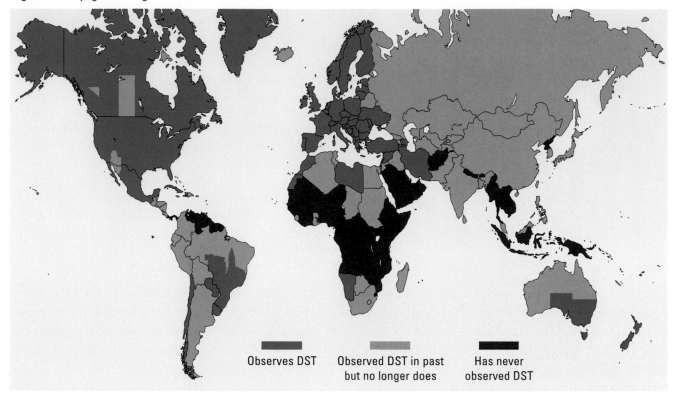

Observes DST   Observed DST in past but no longer does   Has never observed DST

But are these claims valid? Although the evidence does point to a beneficial increase in evening physical activity, several studies also reveal negative health effects. They suggest that it can take weeks for our bodies to adjust to the time change. During this period of adjustment, we get tired and are more likely to get sick. We are also less productive. For some people, the time change may represent a more serious health risk. A 2008 Swedish study found people are at a higher risk of heart attack just after the spring-time change, when they lose an hour of sleep. The 8 authors of the study believe this is because the time change disturbs the body's natural rhythms.

These conflicting claims have led many 9 people to wonder whether the extra hour of light in the evening is worth all the trouble. Opinions vary on this matter. It is said that when one Native American heard about this practice, he laughed and asked this question: "If you cut a piece off the top of a blanket, sew it to the bottom, is the blanket longer?" No matter what time the clocks say, the number of hours in the day remains the same.

READING COMPREHENSION

Big Picture

A Choose the best answer for each of the following questions.

1. What is the purpose of paragraph 3?
   a. To show that DST saves money
   b. To explain the origins of DST
   c. To tell a funny story

2. What is the main idea of paragraph 4?
   a. DST has been around for a long time.
   b. DST became important during wartime.
   c. DST was established in order to save energy.

3. What is the main idea of paragraph 6?
   a. DST saves energy.
   b. The impact of DST on energy savings is not clear.
   c. DST does not save energy.

4. What is the purpose of paragraph 7?
   a. To show the connection between daylight and safety
   b. To offer an alternative justification for DST
   c. To explain the economics of DST

5. What is the main idea of paragraph 8?
   a. DST has health benefits, but it can also cause health problems.
   b. The health effects of DST are a result of changes in our body's rhythms.
   c. We don't understand the health effects of DST.

6. What is the purpose of the short extra reading, "A Clever Phrase," on page 29?
   a. To provide historical information about Daylight Saving Time
   b. To explain a way of remembering how to change our clocks
   c. To explain the different parts of speech for the words *fall* and *spring*

B Every author has a purpose for writing an article. Read the list below and check (✓) the author's purpose for writing Reading 1.

_____ 1. To show the funny side of DST

_____ 2. To question the reasons for DST

_____ 3. To encourage the adoption of DST

_____ 4. To show the scientific basis of DST

Close-Up

A List four of the benefits of daylight saving time mentioned in Reading 1.

1. _____

2. _____

3. _____

4. _____

B Compare answers to Exercise A with a partner. How strong is the evidence that the author provides for each benefit?

Reading Skill

Understanding the Writer's Perspective

Many academic texts present facts in an objective way. Sometimes, however, the writer expresses a point of view, or perspective, about the topic. You may have to infer this point of view, that is, reach a conclusion from the information you have. In other words, the writer may not state it directly. It is important to recognize when a writer is offering his or her own perspective.

A writer may signal perspective in a variety of ways:

1. By using questions to create doubt in the reader's mind

2. By presenting evidence for the opposite view but then showing why this evidence is either wrong or not persuasive

3. By using quotations that support his/her point of view

4. By using evaluative words and expressions such as *negative, positive, it is (not) clear/useful/productive/logical/helpful*, and so on.

Ⓐ Follow the steps below to find signals for the writer's perspective in Reading 1.
- Reread Reading 1.
- Underline at least one example of each of the four signals listed in the skill box.
- Write the paragraph number.

1. Question: paragraph _____

2. Evidence for the opposite view: paragraph _____

3. Quotations that support the writer's point of view: paragraph _____

4. Evaluative words and expressions: paragraph _____

B Compare answers to Exercise A with a partner. Then check (✓) the statement that you think best reflects the writer's perspective in Reading 1.

_____ **1.** The writer is a supporter of DST.

_____ **2.** The writer questions the benefits of DST.

VOCABULARY PRACTICE

Academic Vocabulary

A Find the words in bold in Reading 1. Use the context to help you match sentence parts to create definitions.

1. If two things are **equivalent** (Par. 3), _____ .

2. If something is **mandatory** (Par. 4), _____ .

3. To **conserve** (Par. 4) something is _____ .

4. A **justification** (Par. 5) is _____ .

5. To **contradict** (Par. 6) something is _____ .

6. **Consumption** (Par. 6) is _____ .

7. To **promote** (Par. 7) something is _____ .

8. If something is **valid** (Par. 8), _____ .

a. a reason for doing something

b. it is based on truth

c. the amount of something that is used or eaten

d. they are about the same

e. to encourage or increase it

f. to use it carefully so it will last

g. it is required

h. to say that it is incorrect

B Choose an academic word from Exercise A that can go on both lines to make a frequently used combinations of words. The first one is done for you.

1. to _____promote_____ the **growth**   to _____promote_____ the **development**

2. primary _____ for   no _____ for

3. a(n) _____ **test**   a(n) _____ **meeting**

4. a(n) _____ **point**   a(n) _____ **claim**

5. to _____ the **research**   to _____ the **findings**

6. to _____ **energy**   to _____ **resources**

7. a(n) _____ **amount**   a(n) _____ **number of**

8. **energy** _____   **food** _____

C Choose a phrase from Exercise B to complete each of the following sentences. You may need to change a word form. In some cases, more than one answer is possible.

1. The distribution of money is fair to everyone. Each school receives a(n) _____ in order to provide after-school programs.

2. It was a surprise that the results of the latest study _____ of an earlier study.

3. International aid will _____ of new industries in the area.

4. The speaker made a(n) _____ about the problem with the plan for new buildings in the neighborhood.

5. Turning off lights and appliances when you leave the house will

_____ .

6. The _____ for the tax increase is that the government needs money to pay for important programs.

7. If you want to lose weight, you need to reduce your _____ .

8. There will be a(n) _____ for all employees at 12:00. Anyone who misses it will lose a day of pay.

Multiword Vocabulary

Ⓐ Find the words in bold in Reading 1. Then write the words that come before and/or after them to complete the multiword vocabulary.

1. _____ _____ **proposal** (Par. 3)

2. on a national _____ (Par. 4)

3. followed _____ (Par. 4)

4. _____ **year** _____ (Par. 4)

5. _____ **crimes** (Par. 7)

6. are _____ _____ _____ **risk** _____ (Par. 8)

7. is worth all _____ _____ (Par. 9)

8. _____ **matter** _____ (Par. 9)

Ⓑ Complete the following sentences with the correct multiword vocabulary from Exercise A. Use the information in parentheses and the context from Reading 1 to help you. In some cases, you need to change the verb form.

1. If you want to compete in the Olympics, you need to train _____ (throughout the year).

2. If you smoke, you may _____ (be in greater danger of) developing many diseases.

3. _____ (it makes no difference what) I do, I can never remember my password.

4. In general, men are more likely than women to _____ (break the law).

5. The committee will _____ (suggest a plan) to build a park next year.

6. Denmark has adopted wind power _____ (across the country).

7. Cooking is not _____ (important enough to make the effort). I would rather just eat a sandwich.

8. One son joined the army and, two years later, her other son _____ (did the same thing).

SAVING DAYLIGHT

"Good-bye, Uncle, see you next Spring"

SET YOUR CLOCK BACK ONE HOUR AT 2 A.M. SUNDAY OCTOBER 27ᵀᴴ

Use the Vocabulary

Write answers to the following questions. Use the words in bold in your answers. Then share your answers with a partner.

1. If you were asked to **make a proposal** to reduce **consumption** of natural resources, what steps would you suggest?

2. What do you do in your own home to **conserve resources** such as water and energy?

3. Do you think recycling **is worth the trouble**?

4. Many schools have begun to **promote** service learning—that is, they want students to learn from serving others in their community. Do you think this is a **valid** idea, or should students concentrate on their academic work?

5. Do you think national service—for example, volunteering in hospitals, parks, or the military—should be **mandatory** for young people?

6. If you saw someone **commit a crime**, would you report it?

7. Some people **are at a higher risk of** getting cancer because of their personal habits. What habits may result in cancer?

THINK AND DISCUSS

Work in a small group. Use the information in the reading and your own ideas to discuss the following questions.

1. **Evaluate.** Do you think the reasons for daylight saving time are valid?

2. **Analyze.** The original justification for DST related to conservation of energy. In what ways has this changed? What might be some reasons for this change?

3. **Give an opinion.** If your community observes DST, do you believe it is worthwhile? If it does not observe DST, do you think it would be a good idea?

4. **Relate to personal experience.** Would you rather wake up and go to work or school in the dark, or come home when it is dark? Explain your reasons.

Academic Vocabulary

to align	to institute	a revolution
to drift	interest	solar
a flaw	precise	

Multiword Vocabulary

all at once	to have something in
to be a step forward	common
to consist of	a leap year
to fall in love with	to make up for lost time
	a prison sentence

Reading Preview

A **Preview.** Read the title as well as the subheadings in Reading 2 on pages 38–40. Then discuss the following questions with a partner or in a small group.

1. What is the problem that the reading describes?

2. What do you think the solution will be?

B **Topic vocabulary.** The following words appear in Reading 2. Look at the words and answer the questions with a partner.

accurate	century	harvest
ancient	culture	lunar
annual	decades	modern
astronomers	festival	revolve

1. Which words relate to the calendar?

2. Which words make you think the reading might be about history?

3. Which words make you think the reading might be about science?

C **Predict.** What do you think this reading will be about? Discuss each word in Exercise B and predict how it may relate to the reading.

Why do we have twelve months in the year? Why do we have 365 days in the year (and sometimes, 366)? Read about the origins and history of the calendar that most of the world uses today.

In Search of an
Accurate
Calendar

The Standing Stones of Callanish, Scotland.
Built nearly 5,000 years ago, the stones may
have been used as a kind of lunar calendar.

What do 19th-century opera composer Gioachino Rossini, Canadian hockey player Cam Ward, Olympic swimmer Cullen Jones, and actor Dennis Farina have in common? Like about five million other people, they have a birthday only every four years. They were born on February 29. That is the day that is usually added to the end of February every four years—that is, every leap year—to align the modern calendar with Earth's revolution around the sun. February 29 is leap day. Leap day is a little trick that the world uses to make up for lost time. It is a trick with a long and complicated history.

The Quarter-Day Problem

Although we think of a year as 365 days, the actual revolution of Earth lasts a little bit longer than that. In fact, Earth revolves around the sun every 365.242 days. This gap between the

Julius Caesar, who introduced the leap year to the Roman Empire

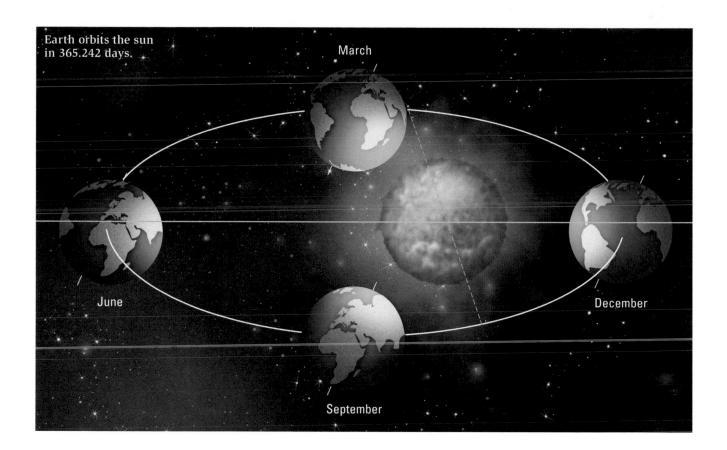

Earth orbits the sun in 365.242 days.

March

June

December

September

calendar year and Earth's revolution has prompted cultures since ancient times to add extra days, or even months, in an effort to align them.

Many early calendars were not very accurate. 3 Our current calendar is based on a solar year, which consists of the 365 days it takes Earth to go around the sun. In contrast, many ancient calendars were based on lunar months, which are about 29.5 days. A year of twelve such months totals only about 354 days. This is about 11 days short of the time it takes Earth to go around the sun. As a result of this difference, annual events soon drifted out of alignment with the seasons. A harvest holiday might come just as farmers were planting; a winter festival day might fall in the spring.

Such inaccuracy was unacceptable during 4 the Roman Empire. The Romans required a precise calendar for business and government. Rent on property, interest on loans, and prison sentences all depended on the calendar. They

"A harvest holiday might come just as farmers were planting; a winter festival day might fall in the spring."

tried to correct the calendar in about 700 BCE[1] by changing the number of days in each month and adding two months—January and February—to their year. These changes helped, but they did not solve the problem. In fact, a long-term solution for the Romans had to wait for a famous love story.

Love Brings Reform to the Roman Calendar

Reform came to Rome via the 5 Egyptians, who were among the first to establish the true length of the solar year. By around 300 BCE, Egypt had adopted a leap-year system. More than three centuries later, the Egyptian ruler Cleopatra fell in love with Julius Caesar. She introduced him to the concept of the leap year, which he brought back to Rome. In 46 BCE, Caesar ordered one 445-day year to correct the decades of drift

---

[1] *BCE:* abbreviation for *before the Common Era.* It indicates the number of years before year 1 of the calendar used in Europe and the Americas.

all at once. Then he instituted the new Julian calendar (named after himself), which had 12 months and 365 days. Every four years, one day was added to the end of the year, which, at that time, was in February.

The new calendar was a tremendous step 6 forward, but it was still not accurate. By the sixteenth century, astronomers realized there was a significant flaw. The solar year is precisely .242 days longer than a calendar year. That is just short of a quarter of a day (4 x .242 = .968). As a result, adding an entire extra day every four years is a slight overcorrection. In other words, leap day adds a little bit too much time—11 minutes too much—every year. Over time, this resulted in an extra day every 128 years. So, by the late 16th century, the Julian calendar had drifted by 10 days.

To resolve this problem, in 1582, Pope 7 Gregory XIII instituted the Gregorian calendar. As in the Julian calendar, a leap year occurs every four years, but there is one exception. It occurs in the first year of the century—years ending in 00—only every four centuries. Thus, while the years 2000 and 2400 are leap years, 2100, 2200, and 2300 are not (see Figure 1). The Gregorian calendar was gradually adopted by much of the world and remains in common use. It finally resolved the problem of aligning the calendar with the revolution of the sun.

Figure 1. Is This a Leap Year?

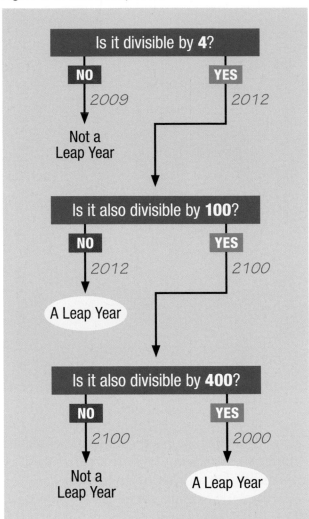

Pope Gregory XIII at a meeting to reform the calendar in 1582

READING COMPREHENSION

Big Picture

Ⓐ The following statements are the main ideas of some of the paragraphs in Reading 2.
Write the correct paragraph number next to its main idea.

_____ **1.** The Romans introduced changes that made the calendar somewhat more accurate.

_____ **2.** The calendar problem was resolved by skipping three leap days every 400 years.

_____ **3.** After learning about it from the Egyptians, Julius Caesar adopted the leap-year system.

_____ **4.** Even after the adoption of leap years, the calendar was not exact.

_____ **5.** Early calendars based on lunar months were not very accurate.

Ⓑ Write a sentence that expresses the main idea of the *whole* reading.

_____

Close-Up

Ⓐ Choose the best answer for each of the following questions, according to the reading.

1. The solar year is _____.
  a. 365 days
  b. a little less than 365 days
  c. a little more than 365 days

2. The lunar year is _____.
  a. eleven days shorter than the solar year
  b. almost 30 days shorter than a solar year
  c. about a quarter of a day longer than a solar year

3. The length of a solar year is related to the movement of _____.
  a. the sun
  b. the moon
  c. Earth

4. During the Roman Empire, an accurate calendar was needed for _____.
  a. religious purposes
  b. business and government
  c. agriculture

5. The addition of _____ to the Roman calendar was an early improvement to the calendar.
  a. two months
  b. an extra day
  c. a leap year

6. Julius Caesar was the one who began the _____ year.
  a. 365-day
  b. 445-day
  c. Julian

7. The Julian calendar was _____.
   a. lunar
   b. accurate
   c. not accurate

8. The Gregorian calendar was _____.
   a. simple
   b. accurate
   c. not accurate

B Use Figure 1 on page 40 to calculate the answers.

1. Calculate the next year that is divisible by four that will *not* be a leap year. _____

2. Calculate the next year that is divisible by 100 that *will* be a leap year. _____

Reading Skill

Creating Time Lines

A time line is a graphic organizer that shows events in the correct order. Creating a time line can help you understand a reading better. For example, some texts contain historical information about events that took place across a period of time. However, the text may not present the events in the order in which they occurred. Making a time line will help you see the sequence of events.

When you create a time line, write very brief notes. If the text provides a date, include it next to the event. If there is no date, just put the events in the order they happened.

A Refer to Reading 2 and number the events below to show the correct order.

_____ **1.** Julius Caesar introduced leap years into the calendar.

_____ **2.** Egypt adopted a leap-year system.

_____ **3.** Many ancient calendars were based on lunar months.

_____ **4.** Pope Gregory made an important change to the calendar.

_____ **5.** The Romans added two months to improve the accuracy of the calendar.

B Make a time line for the events in Exercise A. Add dates to your time line wherever you can. Use brief descriptions, not whole sentences.

VOCABULARY PRACTICE

Academic Vocabulary

A Find the words in bold in Reading 2. Use the context and the sentences below to help you match each word to its correct definition.

_____ **1.** Be sure to **align** (Par. 1) the paper with the edge of the glass before you press print.

_____ **2.** The moon makes a complete **revolution** (Par. 1) around the Earth about every 27 days.

_____ **3.** Many people believe that **solar** (Par. 3) energy will replace energy from oil and coal in the future.

_____ **4.** The plastic bottle **drifted** (Par. 3) in the water until it washed ashore.

_____ **5.** The drawing is very **precise** (Par. 4) and shows all the smallest details.

_____ **6.** **Interest** (Par. 4) rates are increasing every year.

_____ **7.** The government **instituted** (Par. 5) a new policy for the protection of school children.

_____ **8.** There was a **flaw** (Par. 6) in the design of the building so it collapsed during a storm.

a. extra money that you must pay back when you borrow money

b. movement in a circle around a point

c. exact, accurate

d. officially began

e. related to the sun

f. put in a certain position, usually parallel to something

g. a fault or weakness

h. moved slowly without control

B Read each of the following sentences. One of the words below it is frequently used with the word in bold; the other is not. Choose the best word to complete each sentence.

1. Earth's **revolution** _____ the sun takes a little more than 365 days.
   a. along   **b.** around

2. There are many superstitions about what will happen when all the planets **align** _____ Earth.
   a. with   **b.** to

3. The leaves **drifted** _____ in the wind.
   a. slowly   **b.** quickly

4. The number of homes that use **solar** _____ has been growing.
   a. work   **b.** power

5. This design requires very **precise** _____.
   a. measurements   **b.** decisions

6. The school has **instituted** a(n) _____ for new students.
   a. idea   **b.** program

7. At the end of every month, we have to pay the **interest** on our _____.
   a. apartment   **b.** loan

8. There is a _____ **flaw** in the new cellular phone.
   a. major   **b.** full

Multiword Vocabulary

(A) Find the words in bold in Reading 2. Use the context to help you complete each sentence below.

1. If you **have** something **in common** (Par. 1) with another person, _____.
    a. it is very frequent and usual
    b. you both have or do the same thing

2. A **leap year** (Par. 1) is a year _____.
    a. in which an extra day is added to the calendar
    b. that is added every four years

3. If you **make up for lost time** (Par. 1), you _____.
    a. do something that you could not do before
    b. you forget to do something you wanted to do

4. If something **consists of** (Par. 3) things, _____.
    a. those things are parts of it
    b. those things are all the same

5. **Prison sentences** (Par. 4) are _____.
    a. laws that says who must go to prison
    b. the length of time a person must remain in prison

6. If you **fell in love** (Par. 5) with someone, you _____.
    a. married that person
    b. began to love that person

7. If something happens **all at once** (Par. 5), _____.
    a. it happens at the same time
    b. it happens over and over

8. If something **is a step forward** (Par. 6), _____.
    a. it is an improvement
    b. it will be used in the future

(B) Complete the following sentences with the correct multiword vocabulary from Exercise A. Use the information in parentheses to help you. In some cases, you need to change the noun or verb form.

1. This new drug _____ in the treatment of cancer. (It is a much better treatment than what was available in the past.)

2. During the storm, we weren't able to do any work, so now we are _____ by working 14 hours a day. (We could not get that work done before.)

3. The judge gave the young man a short _____. (She sent him to jail for two months.)

4. The couple _____ when they were students and got married after they graduated. (They have loved each other since they were in school together.)

5. The two men _____. They both love football and politics. (They share some interests.)

6. The architect and the project manager decided to have a long meeting so they could take care of remaining problems in the new building _____. (It could happen all at the same time.)

7. The hospital staff _____ six doctors and ten nurses. (There are 16 people on the staff.)

8. Every _____ we add one day to the end of February. (There are 366 days in this year.)

Use the Vocabulary

Write answers to the following questions. Use the words in bold in your answers. Then share your answers with a partner.

1. A **solar** eclipse occurs when the Earth, the sun, and the moon are **aligned**. Have you ever observed a solar eclipse?

2. Does your community follow a lunar or **solar** calendar, or are both calendars **in use**?

3. Sometimes you can buy things at a lower price—such as clothing or dishes—if they contain small **flaws**. Would you rather buy these cheaper products, or do you prefer to buy perfect products at a higher price?

4. Is it important to be **precise** and accurate in your work, or is it more important to get it done quickly? Do you prefer to work on a number of tasks all at once or one at a time? Does it depend on the kind of work? Explain your answers.

5. Find two things that you **have in common** with one or two of your classmates.

6. What is a new rule that your school should **institute**? Why do you think this rule is needed?

THINK AND DISCUSS

Work in a small group. Use the information in the reading and your own ideas to discuss the following questions.

1. **Express an opinion.** How do you think people with leap day birthdays feel about the day? How would you feel if it were your birthday?

2. **Summarize.** Most people find the reasons for having a leap year every four years very confusing. Try to explain it briefly to someone who is not familiar with the information in Reading 2.

3. **Connect to prior knowledge.** Some people believe that leap year is bad luck. For example, in the past, some farmers believed that crops would not grow well in a leap year. Why do you think it has these negative associations?

4. **Connect to prior knowledge.** Are you familiar with any other calendar system? If so, explain it to your group.

Pre-Columbian stone sun calendar

Vocabulary Review

A Complete the reading with the vocabulary below that you have studied in the unit.

align with	in common with	on a large scale	revolution around
consisted of	leap year	precise measurement	slowly drifted
followed suit	major flaw		

The ancient Maya of Central America were famous for their _____ of time
1
and their detailed calendars. The basic elements of these calendars date back to the fifth century

BCE. They were far more accurate than calendar systems that emerged much later in Europe. The

system _____ two different calendar years. The Maya solar calendar had
2
something _____ the modern Gregorian calendar. Like the modern calendar, it
3
had 365 days. The Maya also had a second calendar year with only 260 days. It was used to

determine dates for religious festivals. The Maya had widespread influence, so soon other nearby

communities _____. The calendars were used _____
4   5
throughout the area. However, there was one _____ in the Maya calendar
6
system. Experts do not believe that the Maya system included a(n) _____ every
7
fourth year to account for the extra quarter of a day each year. As a result, this calendar did not

quite _____ Earth's annual _____ the sun. Consequently,
8   9
important dates _____ from one year to another. This may have eventually
10
caused problems for farmers who depended on the calendar to decide when to plant their crops.

B Compare answers to Exercise A with a partner. Then discuss the following questions.

In what ways were the Maya and Roman calendars similar? How were they different?

C Complete the following sentences in a way that shows that you understand the meaning of the words in bold.

1. It **is not worth the trouble** to _____.

2. The government **instituted a program** to _____.

3. _____ **was a** big **step forward** for humans.

4. You can tell that two people have **fallen in love** when _____ .

D Work with a partner and write sentences that include any six of the vocabulary items below. You may use any verb tense and make nouns plural if you wish.

all at once	conserve energy	make up for lost time	solar power
all year round	equivalent amount	primary justification	valid point
be at a higher risk of	make a proposal		

Connect the Readings

A There is a famous saying in English that goes back to at least the 13th century: "Tide and time wait for no man." This saying reflects the widespread belief that human power cannot stop the ocean's tides, and it cannot change or stop time. Nevertheless, throughout human history, we have tried to come up with ideas and inventions to control or manipulate time.

Review Readings 1 and 2. Then, with a partner, fill in the chart below with potential benefits of the inventions and ideas to control time. Use information from the readings and well as your own knowledge.

Invention or Idea	What are the potential benefits?
Accurate calendars	
Accurate clocks	
Daylight saving time	
Leap year	

B Work with your partner or in a small group. Discuss the following questions.

1. In what other ways have humans tried to change or control time? What are the potential benefits?

2. Think of some ways that might be used in the future to measure or control time. Do you think our methods for measuring time might change? For example, a fixed calendar in which dates don't move every year? A metric hour?

C Discuss the following questions with a partner. Use your understanding of the readings and your own ideas.

Many people are fascinated by the idea of time travel. There are many books, films, and television programs that examine this concept.

- Why do you think people find this idea so fascinating?
- Do you think time travel will ever be possible? Explain your answer.
- If so, do you think people of the future are time traveling now?

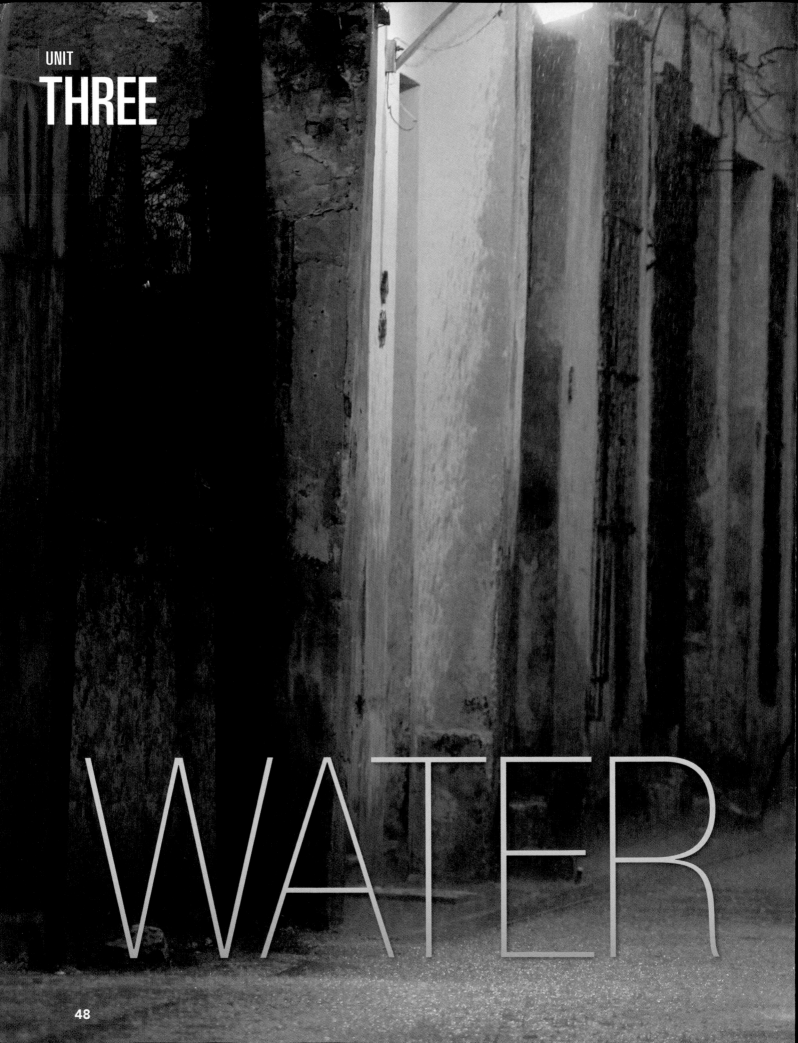

WATER

1. Where does your drinking water come from?

2. Is clean water always available in your community? What would happen if it were not?

A boy dances in water pouring from a gutter during a heavy rainfall in Old Havana, Cuba.

Academic Vocabulary

charity	financial	sanitation
expertise	an obstacle	sparingly
feasible	to participate	

Multiword Vocabulary

to be on board with	in part
to come to a similar conclusion	to make do with
to fall into disrepair	running water
to fall to	spare parts

Reading Preview

A **Preview.** Read the first paragraph and the subheadings in Reading 1. Then discuss the following questions with a partner or in a small group.

1. What do you think Binayo's life is like?
2. What kinds of costs might be connected to "fetching water"?
3. What do you think a "water aid project" is?

B **Topic vocabulary.** The following words appear in Reading 1. Look at the words and answer the questions with a partner.

accessible	fetch	productive
construction	machinery	shallow
crucial	overwhelming	sustainable
drill	precious	well

1. Which words relate to water?
2. Which words are about building?
3. Which words are adjectives? What do they mean?

C **Predict.** What do you think this reading will be about? Discuss each word in Exercise B and predict how it may relate to the reading.

We use water every day: for drinking, cooking, and washing. Most of us can use as much water as we want. Come visit a world where water is much more limited and precious.

Drinking Water

Villagers in Foro, Ethiopia, carry river water for drinking and cooking.

Aylito Binayo knows the mountain trail. Even at four in the morning, she can run down to the shallow river with just the light from the stars. Then she climbs the steep mountain back up to her village with 50 pounds of water (22.5 kilos), sometimes even 100 pounds of water (46 kilos), on her back. She has made this journey several times a day since she was a young girl. When she was eight years old, Binayo left school, in part, to help her mother fetch water from the river. Its water is dirty and unsafe to drink, but it is the only water the Ethiopian village has.

Like Binayo in Ethiopia, nearly a billion people have no access to clean water. Almost half of the world's population lacks running water in their homes (see Figure 1). Dirty water and lack of sanitation kill 3.4 million people around the world annually. Most of them are children under the age of five.

The Cost of Fetching Water

Where clean water is scarce, fetching it takes an enormous amount of time and energy. Women like Binayo spend about eight hours a day on the task, making as many as five trips up and down the mountain. International organizations estimate that this adds up to 200 million hours of labor a day around the world—hours that could be spent more productively.

All of this work makes water very precious, so villagers use it very sparingly. Aylito Binayo makes do with only two and a half gallons a day (9 liters). In contrast, the average American home uses 350 gallons (1,325 liters) of water every day. It is difficult to persuade villagers to use their water for washing when they have to carry each gallon. And yet good hygiene matters. Proper hand washing can reduce waterborne diseases[1] by up to 45 percent. Binayo washes her hands about once a day; she washes her body much less frequently. She washes clothes once a year. "We don't even have enough water for drinking. How can we wash our clothes?" she asks.

Clean, accessible water can transform a community. It is crucial in helping people live healthier and more productive lives. With easy access to water, their daily lives change dramatically. With all the hours they previously spent fetching water,

4

> *"Almost half of the world's population lacks running water in their homes."*

people can grow more food, raise more animals, or even start businesses. In addition, when they can wash frequently and drink clean, safe water, they get sick less often. They also spend less time caring for family members who are sick. Finally, accessible, clean water means children do not have to spend their time fetching water. Instead, they can go to school and look forward to a better life.

Successful Water Aid Projects

The task of supplying water to remote villages is vast and sometimes overwhelming. It often involves large projects that cost a lot of money. Safe drinking water usually requires a well.[2] To drill a well is especially challenging in mountainous areas, where the water table[3] may be far below the surface. Yet, even in areas where

6

---

[1] *waterborne diseases:* diseases that are carried by or through water

[2] *well:* a hole that is dug deep in the ground in order to get water

[3] *water table:* the level beneath the surface of the Earth where water can be found

Figure 1. Global Access to Fresh Water in 2011

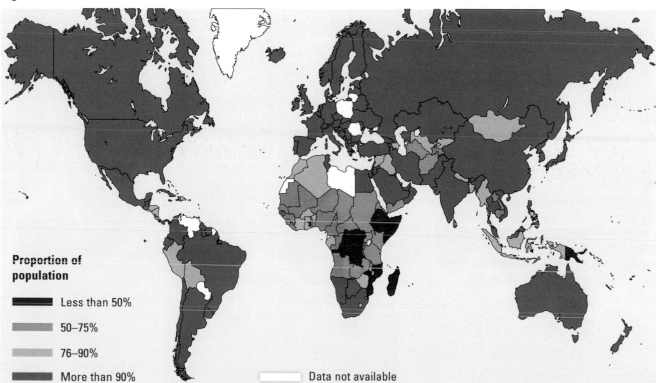

Proportion of population

■ Less than 50%
■ 50–75%
■ 76–90%
■ More than 90%

☐ Data not available

Source: World Health Organization

drilling wells is more feasible, many villages do not have them. This is because drilling holes for wells requires expertise and expensive machinery. Often neither the community nor the government can provide these, so the effort to make clean water accessible falls largely to private and international aid groups.

7   Sadly, however, in many villages like Binayo's, such water projects have failed. In the developing world,[4] about half of all water projects fall into disrepair soon after the aid groups leave. Sometimes the projects use technology that is too difficult for people in the community to manage and repair. In other cases, spare parts are either too expensive or not available. However, the biggest obstacle to the success of these water projects is lack of community involvement. When communities participate in a project from the beginning, they feel a sense of ownership. When residents feel that the project belongs to them, they want the project to succeed, so they work to maintain it. Without such involvement, projects are generally not sustainable.

[4] *developing world:* parts of the world that are poor and have few industries

8   In successful projects, aid groups make sure that the local community participates in designing, building, and maintaining new water projects. To accomplish this, one aid group, WaterAid, asks each community to form a water committee before the group begins any project. The committee then works with WaterAid to plan the project and involve the village in its construction. After WaterAid leaves, the committee maintains and runs the project.

9   Another aid group, Water.org, has come to a similar conclusion about community involvement, but it goes one step further. Water.org's director, Gary White, says that sustainable projects require not just the community members' ideas but also their financial investment. He says that at least 80 percent of the community needs to be on board with the project and to help raise the money to support it. The members of the community need to participate in the project's construction and maintenance. His organization provides loans because he knows that if the villagers' money is invested in a water project, they will take good care of it. That is how a project changes from an act of charity into a valuable and sustainable community resource.

Woman pumps up well water in Sierra Leone, West Africa.

READING COMPREHENSION

Big Picture

A Choose the best answer for each of the following questions.

1. What is the purpose of the first two paragraphs?
   a. To show that water is difficult to carry
   b. To provide facts to support the ideas in the reading
   c. To illustrate the problems of water access with a personal story

2. What is the main idea of paragraph 4?
   a. Water is scarce and used sparingly in some communities.
   b. Good hygiene can save lives.
   c. The developed world and the developing world view water very differently.

3. What does paragraph 5 do?
   a. It argues for access to clean water for people all over the world.
   b. It explains the challenges of providing clean water.
   c. It lists the ways that access to water can improve people's lives.

4. What is the main idea of paragraph 7?
   a. Many water projects fail because the machinery falls apart too quickly.
   b. Water projects require community participation in order to be successful.
   c. Often communities do not maintain water projects.

5. What important idea does paragraph 9 add to the previous ideas in the reading?
   a. The significance of a community's financial investment
   b. The problems of water aid projects
   c. Factors in sustainability of aid projects in developing countries

B Write a sentence that expresses the main idea of the *whole* reading.

Close-Up

A Decide which of the following statements are true or false according to the reading. Write *T* (True) or *F* (False) next to each one.

_____ 1. Half of the world's population lacks access to clean water.

_____ 2. Hand washing can cut the rate of disease caused by dirty water almost in half.

_____ 3. Governments are unable to drill all the wells that are needed.

_____ 4. Most water projects built by aid groups have been very successful.

_____ 5. Water committees often run water projects very successfully.

_____ 6. Aid organizations have found that their projects are most successful when the organizations maintain them themselves.

B Work with a partner or in a small group. Change the false statements to make them true.

Reading Skill

A In the following paragraph, underline signal words of implicit conditions and the sentences that express implicit conditions.

> After big storms, people often have to live without power for a while. Whenever storms cause a lot of wind damage, large branches of trees are likely to break and fall. When they fall on the wires and cables that carry electricity, the result is often a loss of electrical power. Even in major cities, it can often take days or even weeks before these services are restored. After Hurricane Sandy hit the east coast of the United States in 2012, many people continued to live in their cold, dark homes for weeks. They said it was difficult to live with no power. However, they said water was even more important. Without water, it is impossible to live a normal life.

B Look back at Reading 1 and find each event or action listed in the last column of the chart below. Then write the condition for each event or action in the middle column. Finally, in the first column, write the signal word in the reading that implicitly signals each condition.

Signal Word	Condition	Event or Action That May Occur Under This Condition
where	*water is scarce*	fetching water takes a lot of time and energy (Par. 3)
		people's lives can change (Par. 5)
		people can grow more food (Par. 5)
		people feel a sense of ownership (Par. 7)
		people work to maintain the project (Par. 7)
		projects are not sustainable (Par. 7)

VOCABULARY PRACTICE

Academic Vocabulary

A Find the words in bold in Reading 1. Use the context and the sentences below to help you choose the correct definition.

1. Effective **sanitation** (Par. 2) protects the public's health. If there is garbage everywhere, people get sick.

   a. washing frequently **b.** removal of dirty waste and water

2. His doctor told him to use salt **sparingly** (Par. 4). Eating too much could damage his heart.

   a. carefully **b.** daily

3. After learning of the high cost of the new building, the committee decided that it was not **feasible** (Par. 6) to begin construction until next year.

   a. possible **b.** difficult

4. Because her area of **expertise** (Par. 6) is medical technology, the hospital offered her a job.

   a. knowledge **b.** responsibility

5. The biggest **obstacle** (Par. 7) to the success of the new store is that it is far away from major roads.

   a. something that explains **b.** something that prevents

6. More than 10,000 athletes **participate** (Par. 7) in the Olympics every four years.

   a. take part **b.** benefit

7. The president predicted good **financial** (Par. 9) news for next year. Everyone will have more money to spend.

   a. economic **b.** political

8. After the earthquake destroyed their homes, many families had to rely on **charity** (Par. 9) for food.

   a. aid organizations **b.** political organizations

B Choose an academic word from Exercise A that can go on both lines to make frequently used combinations of words. The first one is done for you.

1. **use** _____*sparingly*_____   **eat** something _____*sparingly*_____

2. _____ **fully**   _____ **actively** in something

3. _____ **assistance**   _____ **support**

4. **technical** _____   **professional** _____

5. to be **economically** _____   to be **politically** _____

6. the **main** _____   a **major** _____ **to**

7. **basic** _____   **poor** _____

8. to **give** money to _____   to **contribute** to _____

C Complete the following sentences with your own ideas. Use bold words from Exercise B that the academic words below often appear with. More than one word is possible. In some cases, you need to change the word form.

1. _____ **sanitation** is a factor in _____ .

2. All of the students have **participated** _____ in _____ .

3. This will require **financial** _____ from _____ .

4. It is not clear whether it will be _____ **feasible** to _____ .

5. The _____ **obstacle** to success is _____ .

6. People who _____ to **charity** _____ .

7. _____ recommend that people _____ this **sparingly**.

8. We will need considerable _____ **expertise** in order to _____ .

Multiword Vocabulary

A Find the multiword vocabulary in bold in Reading 1 and use the context to help you figure out the meaning. Then match each item to the correct definition.

_____ 1. **in part** (Par. 1)

_____ 2. **running water** (Par. 2)

_____ 3. **makes do with** (Par. 4)

_____ 4. **falls to** (Par. 6)

_____ 5. **fall into disrepair** (Par. 7)

_____ 6. **spare parts** (Par. 7)

_____ 7. **come to a** similar **conclusion** (Par. 9)

_____ 8. to **be on board with** (Par. 9)

a. decide that something is true

b. to agree with

c. becomes the responsibility of

d. become broken or in bad conditions

e. pieces that replace ones that are broken

f. uses what is available even though it is not enough

g. to some extent, partially

h. water that comes from pipes and a faucet

B Complete the following sentences with the correct multiword vocabulary from Exercise A. In some cases, you need to change the verb form.

1. We can fix the printer as soon as we receive _____ to replace the ones that are broken.

2. Many communities in the developing world do not have access to

   _____.

3. Both researchers _____: More data was needed before they could publish a report.

4. A person's success depends on intelligence and hard work but also,

   _____, on luck.

5. Finally after a long meeting, everyone _____ the plan for the new building. It was approved.

6. Many families left town after the terrible storm and soon their homes

   _____.

7. There is no more milk so the children will have to _____ water.

8. The president is in charge of major decisions in the company, but the details of the operation _____ the vice-president.

Use the Vocabulary

Write answers to the following questions. Use the words in bold in your answers. Then share your answers with a partner.

1. Who is responsible for providing water and **sanitation** services in your community?

2. Do you think you could **make do without running water**? For how long?

3. What social services (for example, programs to help people who cannot afford to buy healthy food for their families) do you think are the government's responsibility? Which services should **fall to charity** organizations? Give reasons for your answers.

4. Have you ever **participated in** a charity or aid project? Did you provide your **expertise** or **financial support**? Did you volunteer your time? Explain your answer.

THINK AND DISCUSS

Work in a small group. Use the information in the reading and your own ideas to discuss the following questions.

1. **Apply knowledge.** Imagine you had to live without running water. How would your life change? What tasks would be the most difficult?

2. **Make connections.** How is access to water and sanitation related to economic development? How can lack of access to water become an obstacle to development?

3. **Suggest solutions.** If you wanted to help a community like the one described in the reading, what do you think would be the best strategy?

Academic Vocabulary

alarming	to ban	to transport
an alternative	a debate	vigorous
to appreciate	portable	

Multiword Vocabulary

to be up to someone	to quench one's thirst
health food	to take sides
in this light	to take up space
pros and cons	worst of all

If you drink bottled water, you are not alone. Read about the growing use of bottled water and then decide for yourself: Is bottled water good or bad?

Reading Preview

A **Preview.** Read the second paragraph in Reading 2 on page 62. Skim the rest of the reading for about one minute. Then discuss the following questions with a partner or in a small group.

1. What are the two "sides" in the reading?
2. Where might you find a reading like this?
3. How is it different from other readings in this book?

B **Topic vocabulary.** The following words appear in Reading 2. Look at the words and answer the questions with a partner.

benefits	healthy	refreshing
consumers	landfill	reliable
convenient	plastic	tax
costs	recycled	waste

1. Which words are connected to money?
2. Which words relate to environmental concerns?
3. Which words can be used for things that are positive and desirable?

C **Predict.** What do you think this reading will be about? Discuss each word in Exercise B and predict how it may relate to the reading.

A long-tailed macaque drinks from a stolen water bottle in Bali, Indonesia.

The
Bottled-Water
Debate

THE BOTTLED-WATER DEBATE

Water is everywhere in our lives. We 1 bathe in water, we wash dishes with water, we swim in water, but, most important, we drink water. In much of the developed world, people get their drinking water from the faucet—that is, tap water. Tap water is generally safe and free. In recent years, however, more and more people have been turning to bottled water as their source of drinking water. The United States is the biggest consumer of bottled water, but China, Mexico, and Brazil are not far behind (see Table 1). This trend has fueled a vigorous debate about the pros and cons of bottled water. Some communities have taxed or even banned the sale of bottled water. Others defend their right to choose what kind of water they drink. It seems that everyone is taking sides.

What are the issues? Below are 2 two points of view that appeared in a national newspaper. J.B., the leader of a U.S. environmental group, argues against bottled water. Next, A.R., the president of a company that sells bottled water, tells her side.

Table 1. Global Bottled Water Consumption 2009 (in billions of gallons)

Country	Annual Consumption	Country	Annual Consumption
United States	8.45	Indonesia	2.94
Mexico	6.89	Germany	2.84
China	5.69	France	2.16
Brazil	4.25	Thailand	1.74
Italy	2.81	Spain	1.27

Source: Beverage Marketing Corporation

J.B. There are many reasons not to buy 3 bottled water, but first let's look at the reasons to drink tap water. In the developed world, tap water is safe and healthy because the government sets standards for safe drinking water. It also costs almost nothing. In New York, officials estimate that you would pay 2,900 times more for bottled water than for the same amount of tap water.

Bottled water also has hidden costs. Today 4 bottled water is shipped all over the world—from France to California, from Italy to Australia, and from Fiji to Germany—at an enormous cost. In the United States alone, about a billion bottles of water are transported around the country every week. Water is heavy so trucks and trains carrying water use a lot of fuel. Surprisingly, bottled water also wastes water. It takes three liters of water to produce one liter of bottled water. Worst of all is what happens after you finish drinking the water. Where do all of those bottles go? Americans alone throw away 38 billion plastic water bottles every year and fewer than 25 percent of them are recycled. Most of them end up in landfills, where they will remain for years. If everyone went back to drinking tap water, we could resolve this problem quickly.

A.R. We believe that consumers should have the choice of both tap water and bottled water. Bottled water will not replace tap water, but bottled water has many benefits. Most important, consumers appreciate the fact that bottled water is portable. This convenient feature makes it easier to take water wherever you go. This can lead to an increase in water consumption, which is important for maintaining good health. 5

There are other health benefits. In countries where tap water is either not accessible or it is 6 not safe to drink, bottled water is an important and reliable alternative to tap water. In developed countries, it offers a convenient, healthy alternative to drinks that contain a lot of sugar. The World Health Organization predicts that the number of overweight adults will soon rise to 2.3 billion. Consumption of sweet drinks has contributed to this alarming trend, so it is important that we have bottled water as an option. Seen in this light, bottled water can be considered a health food. Water is, quite simply, the healthiest and most refreshing way to quench your thirst.

We take our environmental responsibility very seriously. Plastic water bottles are made primarily from recycled material, and, every year, we are finding ways to make our bottles thinner so they take up less space when they are thrown away. In addition, recycled bottles can be transformed into a wide range of useful items including park benches, playground equipment, even textiles. It is up to consumers to make sure that their water bottles do not end up in landfills. Bottled water is a healthy and responsible choice, and consumers have the right to make that choice. 7

READING COMPREHENSION

Big Picture

A Write the main idea for the following paragraphs in Reading 2. Use the words in the box to help you.

bottled water	harmful	inexpensive	safe
convenient	healthy	recycled	tap water

1. Paragraph 1: _____

2. Paragraph 3: _____

3. Paragraph 4: _____

4. Paragraph 5: _____

5. Paragraph 6: _____

6. Paragraph 7: _____

B Write a sentence that expresses the purpose of the *whole* reading.

Close-Up

A Scan Reading 2 to find the answers to the following questions. Write short answers.

1. How much bottled water was consumed in the United States in 2009? _____

2. After the United States, which two countries consume the most bottled water? _____

3. How many bottles of water move around the United States every week? _____

4. What is the rate of recycling for plastic bottles? _____

5. How much water does it take to produce one liter of bottled water? _____

6. When plastic bottles are recycled, what kinds of products (other than new bottles) can be produced? _____

B Compare answers to Exercise A with a partner. Then discuss the following questions.

1. What environmental concerns are related to the bottled-water debate?

2. Which environmental concern do you think is most important?

Reading Skill

Supporting Details in a Persuasive Text

A persuasive text is piece of writing in which the author tries to convince readers about an issue or point of view. You can find persuasive texts on a newspaper's editorial page or on a blog. Persuasive texts often contain explicit arguments. You may find facts, statistics, and illustrations that support these arguments.

1. A **fact** is something that is generally known to be true.

   The cost of water varies considerably across the world.

2. A **statistic** is a numerical fact.

   Almost three and half million people die every year from water-related diseases.

3. A **written illustration** gives an example that makes a fact easier to understand or visualize.

   That is about the same number of people who live in the cities of Hanoi, Vietnam; Berlin, Germany; or the entire country of New Zealand.

A Read the following paragraph and decide if each sentence contains a fact (*F*), a statistic (*S*), or a written illustration (*I*). Write the appropriate letter on the line after the sentence. If the sentence includes none of these, write *X* in the blank. The first one has been done for you.

Your old cell phone can do a lot of damage if you throw it in the trash. __*F*__
1

A hundred million cell phones are thrown away every year around the world. _____ If
2

you put them in a line, they would go on for almost a thousand miles! _____ Cell phones
3

contain dangerous metals and chemicals that may leak and cause harm. _____ Some
4

of the parts and metals in old phones can be recycled or reused. ____ Unfortunately,
5

only about 10 percent of phones are recycled. ____ Be responsible: Recycle your
6

phone! ____
7

B For each of the two positions presented in Reading 2, find the reasons that each
person offers. Briefly state the reasons. If the person supports the reason with a fact
(*F*), statistic (*S*), or written illustration (*I*), write the letter(s) in parentheses after the
reason. The first one has been done for you.

J.B.:
For tap water:

1. *It is healthy. (F)* _____

2. _____

Against bottled water:

1. _____

2. _____

3. _____

A.R.:
For bottled water:

1. _____

2. _____

3. _____

VOCABULARY PRACTICE

Academic Vocabulary

A Find the words in bold in Reading 2. Use the context to help you match each word to
the word or phrase that is closest in meaning.

____ 1. **vigorous** (Par. 1)	**a.** frightening
____ 2. **debate** (Par. 1)	**b.** a different choice
____ 3. **banned** (Par. 1)	**c.** understand how good something is
____ 4. **transported** (Par. 4)	**d.** easy to carry
____ 5. **appreciate** (Par. 5)	**e.** using a lot of energy
____ 6. **portable** (Par. 5)	**f.** prohibited, did not allow
____ 7. **alternative** (Par. 6)	**g.** a discussion between people with different views
____ 8. **alarming** (Par. 6)	**h.** moved goods or people from one place to another

B The academic words in bold on the left often appear with the nouns on the right. Choose nouns from the chart to complete the sentences below. More than one answer is possible for some items. Use the singular or plural form as appropriate.

Academic Words	Nouns
vigorous _____	exercise, debate
portable _____	devices, heaters
alarming _____	news, rate, level
to **transport** _____	goods, supplies, people
to **ban** _____	weapons, smoking, books
to **appreciate** _____	help, support, effort

1. In 1995, California **banned** _____ in public places such as in schools and government offices.

2. **Portable** _____ such as computers and phones have gotten smaller every year.

3. The company uses both trucks and trains to **transport** _____ to their factories.

4. The river has reached an **alarming** _____. Soon there may be a flood.

5. I **appreciate** all of the _____ that my parents provided when I was growing up.

6. It is important to drink a lot of water before **vigorous** _____.

Multiword Vocabulary

A Find the words in bold in Reading 2. Then write the words that come before and/or after them to complete the multiword vocabulary.

1. _____ **and cons** (Par. 1)

2. **taking** _____ (Par. 1)

3. _____ **of all** (Par. 4)

4. **in this** _____ (Par. 6)

5. _____ **food** (Par. 6)

6. _____ **your thirst** (Par. 6)

7. _____ _____ **less space** (Par. 7)

8. **is** _____ _____ **consumers** (Par. 7)

B Complete the following sentences with the correct multiword vocabulary from Exercise A. Use the information in parentheses to help you. In some cases, you need to change the word form.

1. We do not take our bicycles on vacation because they _____ (fill up) in the car.

2. Before you make a decision, it is important to consider all the _____ (benefits and disadvantages).

3. I left my wallet and glasses on the airplane, but, _____ (the most negative thing is), I left my passport.

4. Many people consider yogurt a(n) _____ (a natural product that is good for you).

5. It is important not to _____ (support a position) until you have heard the details of both arguments.

6. It will _____ (be the responsibility of) the employees to make the company successful.

7. _____ (from this perspective), the child's behavior can be considered normal for his age.

8. Coffee and sweet drinks will not _____ (stop you from wanting to drink liquids).

Use the Vocabulary

Write answers to the following questions. Use the words in bold in your answers. Then share your answers with a partner.

1. Some teachers believe that **portable devices** such as cell phones should be **banned** in classrooms. Do you agree or disagree? What are the **pros and cons** of having them in the classroom?

2. If the decision **were up to you**, which devices would you allow in the classroom?

3. Do you enjoy watching political **debates**? Do you usually **take sides** on important issues?

4. What kinds of **health food** do you like to eat? What **health food** do you dislike?

5. Do you **appreciate** it when restaurants list how many calories are in each menu item? Or, do you prefer not to know this information?

THINK AND DISCUSS

Work in a small group. Use the information in the reading and your own ideas to discuss the following questions.

1. **Express an opinion.** Take sides on the bottled water debate. Which side's arguments do you think are more convincing? Explain your answer.

2. **Make an inference.** What can you infer about J.B.'s and A.R.'s values, politics, and lifestyles from their articles on pages 62 and 63?

3. **Predict.** Do you think the popularity of bottled water will increase in the future? Why, or why not?

Vocabulary Review

A Complete the reading with the vocabulary below that you have studied in the unit.

alarming rate	major obstacles	running water	use sparingly
economically feasible	make do with	technical expertise	worst of all
in part	quench their thirst		

It seems that the people of the world cannot _____. They need more and
more water every year. Countries with access to fresh water are digging deeper in the ground to
find water. They are draining their lakes and rivers. Water tables are sinking at a(n)
_____. _____, people in many developed countries do
very little to conserve water.

Not all countries have access to rivers or lakes that can provide lots of fresh water. For some of
them, however, there is an alternative: *desalination*. Desalination is a process that takes the salt
out of seawater and makes it safe for human consumption. However, only about 1 percent of the
world's _____ comes to us as a result of desalination.
_____, this is because desalination is expensive. It requires special
equipment, _____, and, more important, it requires energy. All of these
requirements are _____ for most of the developing world, so that desalination
is not a(n) _____ solution to their water needs. People in these countries
therefore see water as a precious resource that they must _____. Without
alternative water sources, they simply must _____ the traditional sources of
water that they have.

B Compare answers to Exercise A with a partner. Then discuss the following questions.

Do you think there will be increasing reliance on desalination in the future? Why, or why not?

C Complete the following sentences in a way that shows that you understand the
meaning of the words in bold.

1. There has been **vigorous debate** about _____.

2. I don't think _____ is really a **health food** because _____.

3. It **is up to** parents to _____.

4. I prefer to **give money to charities** that _____.

D Work with a partner and write sentences that include any six of the vocabulary items
below. You may use any verb tense and make nouns plural if you wish.

appreciate help	fall to	portable device	take sides
be on board with	financial support	pros and cons	take up space
come to a similar conclusion	participate fully		

Connect the Readings

(A) Think about the ideas in the two readings in this unit. Read the situation and the email message below. Then work with a partner to answer the questions.

Situation: Imagine you are the president of the fictional Djalita Water Company, which sells bottled water from the fictional country of Djaleen. The email message below has been sent out all over the Internet by a group that sees your product in a very negative light. Most of the message contains facts, but you believe that it presents an unfair picture of your company. Because of this message, customers have begun to think badly of your company. Sales of your bottled water are falling. You are very worried about the future of your company.

> **Don't buy Djalita Water!** Djalita Water comes from The Republic of Djaleen, a country with few natural resources. Water is one of them. The Djalita Water Company is taking this precious resource and transporting it all over the world to countries such as the United States, France, and Australia. Yet, half of the people of Djaleen do not have access to running water. And they cannot afford to buy Djalita bottled water. Most Djaleeners have to fetch water from the river, which, in some cases, is more than a mile from their homes. Almost 5 percent of the children of Djaleen die before the age of five, many of them as a result of waterborne diseases. In our own country, people have thrown away more than five billion plastic Djalita water bottles. Most of them ended up in landfills.
>
> Help the people of Djaleen. Help reduce waste in this country. Don't buy Djalita Water!

1. Analyze the message. What are the two arguments that the message makes against the Djalita Water Company?

_____

_____

2. What steps could your company take to change the negative public opinion? You cannot stop using water from Djaleen, but what could you do to lessen the negative impact? Your company is willing to spend some money. Read the two suggestions below. Add specific ideas or details.

   a. Perhaps the company can help the people of Djaleen, especially regarding their access to clean water. Specific suggestions:

   _____

   _____

   b. Perhaps you can do something to show that Djalita cares about the environment in this country? Specific suggestions:

   _____

   _____

(B) In a small group, compare answers to Exercise A. Discuss the differences in your answers.

(C) Discuss the following questions with a partner. Use your understanding of the readings and your own ideas.

1. Should water, like air, be free for everyone? Or, should it be bought and sold, like oil or gas?

2. On the one hand, if water is free, people are likely to waste it. On the other hand, if water costs money, what happens to people who cannot afford it? What is your view?

UNIT
FOUR

TRAVEL

Thrill-seeker Brian Mosbaugh crosses a highline in Smith Rock State Park, Oregon, USA.

FOCUS

1. What kinds of activities do you like to do when you are on vacation?

2. Do you enjoy risky activities?

3. Do you like to go to places that few tourists visit?

Academic Vocabulary

duration	fragile	an option
to emerge	frigid	a thrill
a fatality	a lure	

Multiword Vocabulary

a body of water	in the event of
to come to mind	not a single
to come with the territory	nothing beats
common sense	to run out of

Reading Preview

A **Preview.** Read the title and subheadings in Reading 1. Then discuss the following questions with a partner or in a small group.

1. What do you think *extreme diving* means?

2. What kinds of diving locations do you think will be discussed in the reading?

3. In what ways are these locations different from more typical diving locations?

B **Topic vocabulary.** The following words appear in Reading 1. Look at the words and answer the questions with a partner.

adventure	depth	sharks
ascent	descent	stunning
caves	oxygen	suffer
currents	risk	surface

1. Which five words are most closely related to the sport of diving?

2. Which words make you think that diving would be exciting?

3. Which words make you think diving might be dangerous?

C **Predict.** What do you think this reading will be about? Discuss each word in Exercise B and predict how it may relate to the reading.

A diver explores a sun-lit *cenote*—a deep water-filled hole—in Yucatán, Mexico.

Come explore the challenging and astonishing world of scuba diving in some of the most beautiful places on Earth, from the blue water of the Caribbean to the icy depths of Antarctica.

Extreme Diving

For some people, a vacation of walking around a city looking at historic sites and museums is not an attractive option. What they want is adventure and even danger, so when they go on vacation, they include activities with an element of risk. These thrill seekers may try extreme activities such as mountain climbing, white-water rafting,[1] or skydiving. Others turn to scuba diving, but after a few dives to explore the underwater world of brightly colored fish and ocean life, this activity may lose its thrill.

---

[1] *white-water rafting:* riding in an open boat through dangerous, fast-moving water

For those brave travelers who seek a little more risk in their diving adventures, here are three extreme—and dangerous—possibilities.

Cave Diving

Cave diving is considered one of the world's most dangerous sports. More people have died diving in caves than climbing Mount Everest. Veterans of the sport say, "Danger comes with the territory. There are no injuries. There are only fatalities." Cave diving is a form of penetration diving, which is one of the reasons it is dangerous. In penetration diving, divers enter the water at a specific point and must return to that same

Cave diver in Gran Cenote, Mexico

point when they emerge from the water. This is in contrast to open-water diving, where divers can return to the surface at any location.

In cave diving, divers may have to swim a 3 long way through dark, narrow passages to reach the origin of their dive. Divers may get lost or get stuck in these narrow passages. If they are stuck for too long, they may run out of oxygen. In addition, the caves themselves are fragile and sometimes parts of them collapse, temporarily trapping divers. Consequently, it is crucial to carry enough oxygen during cave dives in the event of a problem that delays a diver's ascent.

Another source of danger is the depth of some 4 caves. In some cave dives, the descent is more than 400 feet (120 meters). Such deep dives require extra caution on ascent. If divers ascend too quickly, they can become sick or suffer a serious and possibly permanent injury. Finally, in many caves, there are unpredictable currents that can sweep away unprepared divers. Some cave dives are more demanding than others, and they require special training and experience. The most challenging caves are often marked with warning signs that tell inexperienced divers to turn back. Popular cave diving locations include Mexico, Belize, and the Bahamas.

Polar Diving

When most people think of scuba diving, a [5] warm tropical body of water usually comes to mind. But many experienced divers claim that nothing beats polar diving for its sheer beauty—and risk. There are polar-diving spots near both the North Pole and South Pole. One of the most popular is McMurdo Sound in Antarctica. Polar diving, or any kind of ice diving, is also a form of penetration diving. Divers cut a hole in the ice and they must return to that same hole when they ascend to the surface. This always adds to the risk of a dive because it adds to the dive's duration. Similar to caves, polar-dive sites can be fragile. Pieces of ice may break off and block a diver's path back to the opening at the surface.

However, the greatest source of danger in [6] polar diving is probably temperature. Divers must wear extensive protective clothing in order to maintain body temperature. Not a single part of their bodies can touch the frigid water. Any skin that comes in contact with the water is likely to get frostbite.[2] The cold also poses problems for the diving equipment, which can freeze and fail at these extreme temperatures.

> *"Some divers, however, want to see the sharks up close, so they prefer to dive without a cage."*

Diving with Sharks

Many of the dangers of extreme diving [7] are the result of the physical environment in which the dives take place. This is not the case in the open, tropical waters of the Caribbean. Here, the danger comes from sharks. Some tour companies offer dives in cages, which protect the divers. Some divers, however, want to see the sharks up close, so they prefer to dive without a cage.

Diving experts say that the [8] danger depends on the type of shark. Some species are quite shy and unlikely to attack humans. Other species are less predictable, but still, these experts say, the number of shark attacks on divers is very low. They say most

---

[2] *frostbite:* dangerous damage to a part of the body as result of being very cold

Diver swims past ice in the Antarctic Peninsula.

Diving with sharks!

of them are the result of human stupidity; for example, if a diver tries to grab the shark's tail or fin. If divers use their common sense, diving with sharks is probably the safest of these three extreme dives.

The Attractions of Extreme Diving

So, why do some people find it difficult to resist the lure of high-risk dives? Most adventure divers agree that they are hooked on the rush of adrenaline[3] they get when they do a dangerous dive. They say they like to challenge themselves with these more difficult dives. They are also drawn to these unique experiences, the kind that few others have had. 9

Most of all, however, they say that with the danger comes awe-inspiring beauty, which is the real thrill. The underwater caves are filled with strange and wonderful rock formations that cannot be seen anywhere else in the world. Beneath the polar ice are stunning ice formations that resemble mountains of crystal. These dives also offer them a rare opportunity to see animals such as sharks or penguins in their natural habitat. Is it worth the risk? Absolutely! 10

_____

[3] *adrenaline:* a chemical that your body produces when you are scared or excited

READING COMPREHENSION

Big Picture

Ⓐ The following statements are the main ideas of some of the paragraphs in Reading 1. Write the correct paragraph number next to its main idea.

_____ **1.** Extremely low temperatures make polar diving risky.

_____ **2.** Extreme diving is exciting and dangerous.

_____ **3.** Human behavior causes most of the problems that occur during shark dives.

_____ **4.** The structure of underwater caves makes them particularly dangerous.

_____ **5.** Extreme dive locations are very beautiful.

B Write a sentence that expresses the main idea of a paragraph not included in Exercise A.

_____

_____

Close-Up

A Decide which of the following statements are true or false according to the reading. Write *T* (True) or *F* (False) next to each one.

_____ **1.** Cave diving is one of the most dangerous sports in the world.

_____ **2.** In penetration diving, divers enter and leave the water at different points.

_____ **3.** The biggest risk in deep dives is that divers may run out of oxygen.

_____ **4.** Polar divers may get trapped by floating pieces of ice.

_____ **5.** Frostbite is a significant risk in polar diving.

_____ **6.** Shark dives generally take place in tropical waters.

_____ **7.** Diving with sharks is usually very dangerous.

_____ **8.** Risk is only one of the attractions of extreme diving.

B Work with a partner or in a small group. Change the false statements in Exercise A to make them true.

Reading Skill

Finding Out Why

When you read a text, it is important to be able to answer the question, "Why?"

Why did something happen?

Why did someone do a particular action?

Why is the situation like this?

There are many different signal words and phrases that can help you find answers to the question, "Why?" They include the following:

Nouns: *cause, reason, result, source*

Verbs: *lead to, result in, come from*

Question words: *why, how*

Connectors: *so, because, as a result, since*

When you see one of these signal words, read what comes before and after it. You should be able to find an answer to the question, "Why?" Sometimes, however, there is no signal word. In these cases, use your overall understanding of the text.

A Write answers to the following questions. Write the signal words or phrases that helped you find the answer. If there are no signal words, write *none*.

1. Why do some people include an element of risk in their vacations? Find one reason.

   They want adventure and even danger.   Signal word or phrase: *so*

2. Why is cave diving dangerous? Find at least three reasons.

   a. _____   Signal word or phrase: _____

   b. _____   Signal word or phrase: _____

   c. _____   Signal word or phrase: _____

3. Why do divers need to carry extra oxygen in caves? Find at least one reason.

   _____   Signal word or phrase: _____

4. Why is polar diving risky? Find two reasons.

   a. _____   Signal word or phrase: _____

   b. _____   Signal word or phrase: _____

5. What makes diving with sharks dangerous? Find two reasons.

   a. _____   Signal word or phrase: _____

   b. _____   Signal word or phrase: _____

B Compare answers to Exercise A with a partner. Did finding the signal words help you understand the reading?

VOCABULARY PRACTICE

Academic Vocabulary

A Find the words in bold in Reading 1. Use the context and the sentences below to help you choose the correct definition.

1. If you have a serious disease, there may be more than one **option** (Par. 1) for treatment.
   a. choice   b. result

2. For most people, it is a **thrill** (Par. 1) to meet a famous movie star or politician in person.
   a. great opportunity   b. something exciting

3. There were six **fatalities** (Par. 2) as a result of the fire. Ten more people had serious injuries.
   a. deaths   b. losses

4. The crowd waited for the president to **emerge** (Par. 2) from the building.
   a. wave   b. come out

5. This glass is very **fragile** (Par. 3) and should be handled very carefully.
   a. breakable   b. expensive

6. The price of the ride depends on its distance and **duration** (Par. 5).
   a. length of time   b. complexity

7. The **frigid** (Par. 6) air made it difficult to start the car in the morning.

    a. very cold   **b.** very dry

8. For many people, the **lure** (Par. 9) of gambling is very powerful. That is why casinos are so successful.

    a. benefit   **b.** attraction

B Choose the correct academic word from the box to complete each of the following sentences. The words in bold can help you because they often appear with the academic word.

duration	emerged	fatalities	fragile	frigid	lure	option	thrill

1. Archaeologists found a skeleton from two million years ago. The bones were **extremely**
_____.

2. When soldiers return home, the **biggest** _____ is seeing their families again.

3. The number of highway **traffic** _____ rises every year, especially during holidays.

4. Some students have enough money to pay for a university education, but, for others, the **best** _____ is to get a loan.

5. Some people cannot **resist the** _____ of online ads that promise great discounts.

6. The best environment for some types of large fish is the _____ **water** off the coast of Alaska.

7. Several patterns _____ **from** the 10-year study of cancer patients.

8. The flu epidemic only lasted from late January to late February—a relatively **short**
_____.

Multiword Vocabulary

A Find the multiword vocabulary in bold in Reading 1 and use the context to help you figure out the meaning. Then match each item to the correct definition.

_____ **1. comes with the territory** (Par. 2)	**a.** a lake or ocean, for example
_____ **2. run out of** (Par. 3)	**b.** is an unavoidable aspect of a job or activity
_____ **3. in the event of** (Par. 3)	**c.** enters one's thoughts
_____ **4. body of water** (Par. 5)	**d.** finish your supply of something
_____ **5. comes to mind** (Par. 5)	**e.** good judgment
_____ **6. nothing beats** (Par. 5)	**f.** it is impossible to find something better than
_____ **7. not a single** (Par. 6)	**g.** no; none
_____ **8. common sense** (Par. 8)	**h.** in case of

B Complete the following sentences with the correct multiword vocabulary from Exercise A.

1. If you keep eating, we will _____ food before we arrive at our destination.

2. _____ person responded to the request to visit residents of the nursing home. This was very disappointing.

3. The largest _____ in the world is the Pacific Ocean.

4. It is a good idea to carry your cell phone with you _____ an emergency.

5. I enjoy eating in restaurants but _____ a home-cooked meal.

6. It is important to use your _____ when you go camping. Be sure the fire is out before you go to sleep and don't leave any food that wild animals might find.

7. What's the first thing that _____ when you see a shark in a movie?

8. This new job requires a lot of travel. I don't like it, but travel _____.

Use the Vocabulary

Write answers to the following questions. Use the words in bold in your answers. Then share your answers with a partner.

1. What images first **come to mind** when you think about your ideal vacation? Do you feel the **lure** of the ocean? The mountains? The excitement of big cities?

2. If you **ran out of** gas on a highway, what would you do? What **options** would you have **in the event of** other emergencies on the road?

3. Ninety percent of the world's **traffic fatalities** occur in developing countries. What do you think some reasons for this statistic might be? How do you think it could be reduced?

4. "**Nothing beats** the **thrill** of _____." Complete the sentence with something that is true for you. Explain why you think so.

THINK AND DISCUSS

Work in a small group. Use the information in the reading and your own ideas to discuss the following questions.

1. **Relate to personal experience.** Would you like to try extreme diving? Which of the three diving experiences appeals to you? Why?

2. **Infer meaning.** The reading quotes one expert, "There are no injuries. There are only fatalities." What do you think he means?

3. **Analyze results.** According to the reading, many people get into trouble because they ignore the signs like the one in the photo on page 75. Why do you think they do this?

Academic Vocabulary

aftermath	to entice	to patronize
to cater	firsthand	volunteer
to ensure	to inject	

Multiword Vocabulary

all in all	in need
to come face-to-face with	in short supply
to give something a try	out of service
how about	to steer clear of

Vacations are for relaxation and fun, right? Most of the time they are, but sometimes people go on vacations for other reasons. Find out about some vacation choices that may surprise you.

Reading Preview

A **Preview.** Read the first sentence of each paragraph in Reading 2. Then discuss the following questions with a partner or in a small group.

1. What do you think *disaster tourism* is?

2. What might motivate people to visit a disaster area on their vacation?

3. Would you ever want to take a vacation to a disaster area?

B **Topic vocabulary.** The following words appear in Reading 2. Look at the words and answer the questions with a partner.

bargain	destruction	tours
beach	economy	tsunami
crowds	flood	vacation
damage	fortune	value

1. Which words do you think are most closely related to travel?

2. Which words are negative, that is, about bad things that might happen?

3. Which words are related to spending money?

C **Predict.** What do you think this reading will be about? Discuss each word in Exercise B and predict how it may relate to the reading.

Tourists take pictures as smoke spews from Mount Etna in Sicily, Italy.

Disaster Tourism

Destruction caused by Hurricane Katrina in Gulfport, Mississippi, USA

A volunteer fixes a house damaged by Hurricane Katrina in 2005.

1   **W**hat do you like to do on vacation? Relax on a beach? Go mountain climbing or fishing? Visit a world-famous museum? How about visiting the site of a recent tsunami? If the last choice strikes you as strange, you probably have never heard of *disaster tourism*. Disaster tourists choose to visit places where natural disasters such as fires, floods, and earthquakes have caused death and destruction. Following the 2004 tsunami in Southeast Asia, tourists went to view the aftermath of the disaster. Similarly, after Hurricane Katrina in New Orleans in 2005, bus tours took tourists to see the flood damage firsthand. Disaster tourism has become so popular that some travel companies now specialize in this kind of vacation.

2   Why do people want to visit communities where there has been widespread damage and terrible loss? Experts who study disaster tourism say the motivation is not the same for everyone. Some people are just curious. When there is a disaster, they want to see what has happened. Others want to learn from the experience of others. However, communities that are struggling to rebuild after a disaster may not appreciate these tourists. Most travel companies that cater to disaster tourists understand this. They recognize the sensitive nature of this kind of tourism. So, they promise that their tours will not add to the suffering of the people in disaster areas.

Instead, they promote the educational value of coming face-to-face with the destruction caused by nature's power. Most important, they are careful to steer clear of all official search-and-rescue efforts.

3   Other disaster tourists are less interested in witnessing the damage. Instead, they are motivated by the desire to help those in need. Tourists can provide indirect assistance to communities affected by disasters by spending money. After a disaster, the number of tourists usually drops, which adds to the community's troubles. This is especially true for areas that are economically dependent on tourism. Thailand and Sri Lanka both experienced a steep drop in tourism following the 2004 tsunami. New Orleans and other communities along the Gulf of Mexico had barely recovered from Hurricane Katrina when there was a disastrous oil spill in 2010. Both events had a negative effect on tourism. Travel to these communities injects much-needed money

into their economies. Experts give two pieces of advice to tourists who want to help in this way. First, visitors should not take their trip until the critical emergency has passed and the area is ready to receive visitors again. Second, they should patronize hotels, restaurants, and shops that are owned by people in the community rather than big international chains. That way, they ensure their money will remain in the community and help the people who need it the most.

Tourists can also have a more direct effect on these communities by visiting the disaster areas as volunteers. Travel professionals refer to this as "voluntourism." Tourists come to help clean up and rebuild homes, businesses, and schools in the disaster area. Again, experts advise that visitors should wait for a few weeks or months after the disaster before arriving. Also, they should volunteer through an organization that understands the community's needs. Voluntourism vacations that are not well organized, on the other hand, are neither successful for the voluntourists nor beneficial for the people they have come to help. 4

There are some final, more practical reasons why some people choose to visit disaster areas for their vacations. They frequently offer very good value. Often tourists are afraid to come to these areas because they think they may be dangerous. What if there is another earthquake? What if the floods return? What if trains and buses are out of service? Maybe food will be in short supply. Some of these fears may be justified; nevertheless, travel 5

professionals say tourists should still consider disaster vacations. Businesses often lower their prices in an effort to entice tourists to return. There are no crowds and so tourists often have hotels and restaurants to themselves. All in all, a disaster vacation can be a terrific bargain. If you decide to give disaster tourism a try, just make sure that your trip will have a positive impact on the community you are visiting. The best examples put the needs of the victims ahead of the needs of tourists.

HAITI AFTER THE EARTHQUAKE

What do disaster victims think of disaster tourists? An aid worker who was in Haiti after the 2010 earthquake wrote this report about how some Haitians felt:

The Haitians are tired of answering questions from journalists and being photographed by tourists. They are even upset about volunteer tourists who have come to help. It is not difficult to understand why. Would you like to answer question after question from a group of visitors during the worst days of your life? Would you like them to take photographs of your family or the pile of bricks that was your house a few weeks ago? And many Haitians who have lost their homes and who don't have a reliable source of food for their families are wondering: Who is providing food and shelter for the volunteers when there is no food and shelter for us?

READING COMPREHENSION

Big Picture

A Reading 2 gives reasons why people visit disaster areas. Check (✓) the four reasons that appear in Reading 2. Write the paragraph number(s) in which they appear.

_____ **1.** They are interested in the power of nature.

_____ **2.** They want to help people who have suffered in the disaster.

_____ **3.** They are studying disasters as part of their education.

_____ **4.** They think it will be an inexpensive place for a vacation.

_____ **5.** They think they can earn money easily there.

_____ **6.** They want to see the destruction.

B Check (✓) the purpose of the reading.

_____ **1.** To present the author's point of view

_____ **2.** To offer information that may be new to readers

_____ **3.** To persuade readers to take action

_____ **4.** To amuse readers

Close-Up

A Choose the best answer for each of the following questions.

1. What is one thing that disaster tourism companies do *not* do?
  a. They promise to be sensitive to communities in disaster areas.
  b. They help tourists understand disasters.
  c. They help with search-and-rescue efforts.

2. What is the most important advice for tourists who want to travel right after a disaster?
  a. Bring money to help people in trouble.
  b. Stay away from official rescue operations.
  c. Only help people when they request it.

3. How should travelers in disaster areas spend their money?
  a. With tour companies that have ethics policies
  b. At international businesses
  c. At local businesses

4. How can tourists provide direct assistance to communities after a disaster?
  a. Go to the community and help residents rebuild after the rescue phase is over
  b. Visit tourist attractions in the disaster area
  c. Send money to help the people in the community to recover

5. Which of the following situations is *not* likely to happen after a natural disaster strikes a tourist attraction?
  a. Transportation services are interrupted.
  b. Prices at hotels and restaurants go down.
  c. Tourism increases.

6. According to the short extra reading, "Haiti after the Earthquake," on page 85, how did some Haitian residents feel about the tourists who came to the island after the disaster?
  a. They were happy to have tourist volunteers come and help them.
  b. They paid no attention to them because they had enough problems of their own to worry about.
  c. They were annoyed by them.

B Look at the photos in Reading 2 on page 84. Discuss the questions with a partner.

1. Tell your partner about a disaster that you are familiar with. When did it occur? What damage did it cause?

2. Has the community recovered from that disaster? How long did it take?

Reading Skill

There are many different ways to show contrast between sentences. You may be familiar with connectors of direct contrast that show opposite ideas, such as *however*:

> She wants to visit Brazil; <u>however</u>, her husband does not.

Not all contrast connectors express such a direct contrast. Some of them have specialized meanings or restrictions.

1. **instead**

    > We didn't go to Brazil; <u>instead</u>, we spent our vacation money on a new roof.

    The sentence or clause before *instead* says what did **not** happen. The sentence or clause that follows *instead* says what **did** happen.

2. **nevertheless**

    > She has always wanted to visit Brazil; <u>nevertheless</u>, she spends all of her vacations in Latvia.

    A reader would expect her to go to Brazil on vacation. *Nevertheless* introduces a surprise that contrasts with a reader's expectation.

3. **on the other hand**

    > Brazil is an exciting place to visit; <u>on the other hand</u>, Chile is also a great travel destination.

    > Brazil is an exciting place to visit; <u>on the other hand</u>, it is awfully hot this time of year.

    On the other hand introduces contrasting information or an alternative.

A For each of the paragraphs in Reading 2 listed below, find the sentence with a sentence connector. Then write the sentence connector and answer the questions. The first one is done for you.

1. **Paragraph 2**   Sentence connector: *instead*

    What doesn't happen? *Visitors don't add to the suffering.*

    What does happen? *They promote education.*

2. **Paragraph 3**   Sentence connector: _____

    What is not true? _____

    What is true? _____

3. **Paragraph 4**   Sentence connector: _____

    What contrasting information or alternative is offered? _____

4. **Paragraph 5**   Sentence connector: _____

    What is the reader's expectation? _____

    How is the expectation contradicted? _____

B Write a sentence about disaster tourism that shows a contrast, using a sentence connector.

VOCABULARY PRACTICE

Academic Vocabulary

Ⓐ Find the words in bold in Reading 2. Use the context to help you match each word to its correct definition.

_____ 1. **aftermath** (Par. 1)   **a.** directly; personally

_____ 2. **firsthand** (Par. 1)   **b.** be a customer; shop at

_____ 3. **cater** (Par. 2)   **c.** people who do work without being paid in order to help others

_____ 4. **injects** (Par. 3)   **d.** improves something by providing money or other kind of support

_____ 5. **patronize** (Par. 3)   **e.** make certain

_____ 6. **ensure** (Par. 3)   **f.** tempt; persuade someone to do something by offering something

_____ 7. **volunteers** (Par. 4)   **g.** provide a group with all the things they need

_____ 8. **entice** (Par. 5)   **h.** the situation that results from a harmful event

Ⓑ Choose an academic word from Exercise A to complete each of the following sentences. Notice and learn the words in bold because they often appear with the academic words. In some cases, you need to change the verb form.

1. She knows about poverty from _____ **experience**. Her family was very poor.

2. She _____ her friend **into** trying the chocolate cake.

3. The _____ **of** the war lasted for many years, and the recovery cost millions of dollars. It took decades to rebuild the cities.

4. The people in my neighborhood prefer to _____ **stores** that are near their homes.

5. The recent news showing our candidate in the lead has _____ some excitement **into** the election.

6. There are all kinds of specialty stores in the area that _____ **to** different kinds of shoppers.

Multiword Vocabulary

Ⓐ Find the words in bold in Reading 2. Then use the words in the box below to complete the multiword vocabulary.

about	all	coming	give	need	service	short	steer

1. **how** _____ (Par. 1)

2. _____ **face-to-face with** (Par. 2)

3. **to** _____ **clear of** (Par. 2)

4. **those in** _____ (Par. 3)

5. **out of** _____ (Par. 5)

6. **in** _____ **supply** (Par. 5)

7. _____ **in all** (Par. 5)

8. **to** _____ **it a try** (Par. 5)

B Complete the following sentences with correct multiword vocabulary from Exercise A. Use the information in parentheses to help you. In some cases, you need to change the verb form.

1. The automatic bank machine was _____ (not working) so we couldn't get any money.

2. _____ (considering everything), business has been very good this year. The company has made a lot of money.

3. Those dogs are very fierce, so it is a good idea to _____ (avoid) them.

4. After the earthquake, the class raised money to help _____ (people who need help).

5. We always eat at the same restaurant. _____ (what do you think about the idea of) trying a different one tonight?

6. A man who was hiking in the woods said he suddenly _____ (met directly, by surprise) a mountain lion.

7. I have never gone skiing before, but I would like to _____ (make an attempt at it).

8. During World War II, coffee was _____ (not available in large enough amounts; hard to get) so many people drank tea instead.

Use the Vocabulary

Write answers to the following questions. Use the words in bold in your answers. Then share your answers with a partner.

1. Many companies use low prices on special items in order to encourage shoppers to **patronize** their stores. Do you think this is a good strategy? Would low prices **entice** you **into** a specific store? **How about** advertisements? Do they influence where you shop?

2. Have you ever **come face-to-face with** a criminal or a dangerous wild animal? What did you do?

3. Do you think giving money to a charity is the best way to help people **in need**? Do you think it is more effective to provide **firsthand** assistance?

4. Have you ever been a **volunteer** in your community? If not, would you like to **give it a try**?

THINK AND DISCUSS

Work in a small group. Use the information in the reading and your own ideas to discuss the following questions.

1. **Make connections.** Do you think that disaster tourism is a new idea? Or, do you think people have always wanted to view the aftermath of disasters? Explain your answer.

2. **Relate to personal experience.** Would you like to visit a disaster area? Which type of disaster tourism appeals to you? Explain your answer.

3. **Take a different perspective.** Consider disaster tourism from the perspective of a disaster victim. How would you feel about this form of tourism?

Vocabulary Review

A Complete the reading with the vocabulary below that you have studied in the unit.

all in all	come with the territory	in short supply	resist the lure
best option	common sense	patronize stores	steer clear of
cater to	extremely fragile		

Some countries cannot _____ of the large profits that they get from

1
tourism. Tourism can be good for a community's economy, but it is not always good for the
environment or local culture. This is particularly true for _____ ecosystems

2
such as islands, beaches, and polar areas. Tourism may also not be good for places where natural
resources, such as energy and water, may be _____. Yet, in some poor

3
countries, governments feel that tourism is their _____ because it helps

4
the economy.

_____, how big are these problems, really? For tourist attractions, don't

5
these problems just _____? Perhaps, but companies that

6
_____ international tourists claim that some attractions have suffered real

7
damage from the increase in visitors. The solution, they say, is *responsible tourism*. First, they
suggest that tourists take steps to reduce their use of energy. Many of these steps are
_____. For example, they should turn off the lights and air conditioner when

8
they leave their hotel. Second, they should _____ that are owned by local

9
people. Finally, they should _____ anyone who wants to sell them objects that

10
are old and may be cultural treasures.

B Compare answers to Exercise A with a partner. Then discuss the following questions.

What problem and solutions are described in Exercise A? Can you think of any other solutions?

C Complete the following sentences in a way that shows that you understand the
meaning of the words in bold.

1. For me, the **biggest thrill** of traveling is _____.

2. The best way to prevent **traffic fatalities** is _____.

3. Last week we **ran out of** _____.

4. **Nothing beats** _____ on a hot summer day.

D Work with a partner and write sentences that include any six of the vocabulary items
below. You may use any verb tense and make nouns plural if you wish.

aftermath of	entice into	not a single	short duration
come face-to-face with	firsthand experience	out of service	those in need
emerge from	in the event of		

Connect the Readings

A In this unit, you have learned about two unusual ways in which some people choose to spend their vacations. Fill in the chart by answering the questions about each reading.

Question	Extreme Diving	Disaster Tourism
What locations (city, country, or continent) are mentioned in the reading?		
What motivates people to take the kind of vacation described in the reading?		
What dangers or discomforts might the visitor experience?		

B With a partner or in a small group, compare your answers to Exercise A. Then mark the locations on the world map. What other unusual places might people go to for extreme diving or for disaster tourism?

C Discuss the following questions with a partner. Use your understanding of the readings and your own ideas.

1. Think about one recent natural disaster. Is the place where it occurred a place that tourists usually visit? Would this be a good location for disaster tourism? Why, or why not?

2. What challenges might visitors face if they visited the area?

Animal-Human
RELATIONSHIPS

A "Project Protection des Gorilles" coordinator helps an orphan gorilla in the Republic of the Congo.

FOCUS

1. How would you describe the relationship between humans and animals?

2. How are our interactions with farm animals different than our interactions with pets? How are they similar?

3. Can wild animals ever become pets? Should they?

Academic Vocabulary

to acknowledge	captivity	a shift
advantageous	inflexible	transformation
aggressive	prosperity	

Multiword Vocabulary

to date back to	to pave the way for
to fit the bill	to rule out
in the presence of	a source of pride
living conditions	a win-win situation

Humans and cows have lived side by side for centuries. What makes their relationship special? Explore their shared history and read about how both sides have benefited.

Reading Preview

A **Preview.** Look at the photos on pages 96–98. Then discuss the following questions with a partner or in a small group.

1. What roles do cattle play in human lives today?

2. Do you think these roles have changed throughout human history? Explain your answer.

3. Do you think these roles are the same in every culture? Explain your answer.

B **Topic vocabulary.** The following words appear in Reading 1. Look at the words and answer the questions with a partner.

agriculture	coexist	graze
ancestors	domestication	herd
archaeological	evidence	plow
characteristics	fertilizer	protein

1. Which five words are most closely related to farms?

2. Which words are most likely to be found in a text about history?

3. Which words are most likely to be found in a scientific text?

C **Predict.** What do you think this reading will be about? Discuss each word in Exercise B and predict how it may relate to the reading.

A sleeping shepherd is licked by one of his young cows in India.

Humans and Cattle:
A Shared History

HUMANS AND CATTLE: A SHARED HISTORY

For the Maasai of Kenya and Tanzania, 1
cattle are everything. This ethnic group of
almost one million people has been cattle
herders for hundreds of years. Cattle provide
much of what the Maasai need for survival. They
use cows' milk, blood, meat, and skins. Their
standard greeting is, "I hope your cattle are well."
Their lives revolve around the care and protection
of their herds. For the Maasai, cattle are a symbol
of wealth and status and a source of pride. A
large herd guarantees a family's prosperity as

well as a man's prospects for marriage. The
Maasai believe that all of the world's cattle are a
gift to them from God and that caring for cattle is
a Maasai responsibility.

Most historians do not believe that cattle were 2
a divine gift, but they acknowledge that cattle
have played a vital role in human lives. The relationship between humans and cattle dates back to
a time when humans hunted the wild ancestors
of today's cows, thousands of years ago. The
transformation from wild animals to animals that

A Maasai family with their goats and cattle in Maasai Mara, Kenya

can coexist with humans is called domestication. Some scholars argue that the domestication of animals, along with the development of agriculture, was the most significant change in human history (see Figure 1). It helped determine what we eat and how we live, and it paved the way for human settlements on a large scale.

3   Many of these same scholars say that among all domesticated animals, cattle may be the most important. For early herders, as for the Maasai, cattle were like a full-service market on four legs. Cows provided them with major sources of protein in the form of milk and meat. Their skins provided leather for clothing and shoes as well as material for building a shelter. Their bones were used to make tools and weapons. Their dung[1] provided both fuel and fertilizer[2] for crops. Cows were also used for transportation and for labor, especially to plow fields. Many of these functions remain important today.

4   How and when did this transformation take place? Based on archaeological evidence, such as bones and art, scholars believe that the domestication of cattle began between 8,000 and 10,000 years ago. The shift in the relationship from hunter-prey to peaceful coexistence probably took many generations.

5   Cows were among the earliest large animals to undergo domestication. Not all animals are so suitable for domestication, however. According to some scholars, certain features rule out the

---

[1] *dung:* solid waste, especially from cows and horses
[2] *fertilizer:* something that is put on land to make plants grow better

Figure 1. The History of Domestication

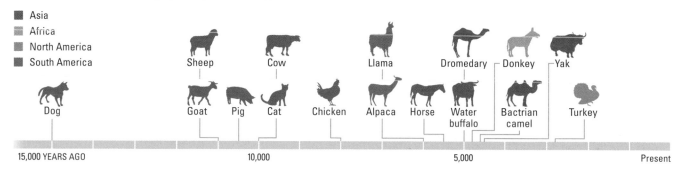

- ■ Asia
- ■ Africa
- ■ North America
- ■ South America

Dog

Sheep   Cow   Llama   Dromedary   Donkey   Yak

Goat   Pig   Cat   Chicken   Alpaca   Horse   Water buffalo   Bactrian camel   Turkey

15,000 YEARS AGO   10,000   5,000   Present

Source: National Geographic Magazine, March 2011

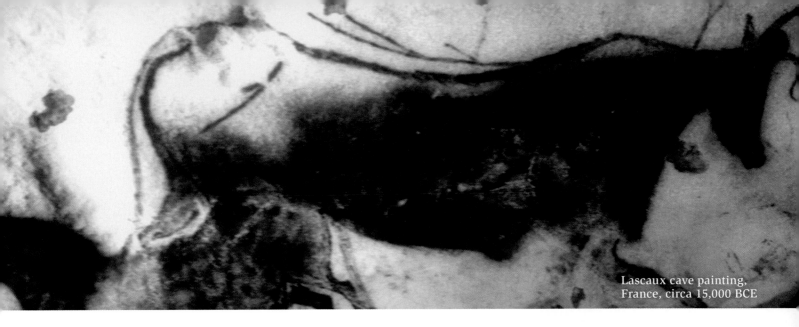

possibility of domestication. If animals display any of these characteristics, they are unlikely to become domesticated:

- They have a flight response.[3]
- They grow very slowly.
- They cannot breed in captivity.
- They have very specific, inflexible requirements for food and living conditions.
- They are very aggressive or likely to attack.

In contrast, animals that live, travel, and graze 6 in herds are ideal for domestication. They feel safe in their herd so they do not immediately run away in the presence of humans. In addition, because they are accustomed to following the leader of their herd, they can accept a human as a substitute for that leader. Based on all of these characteristics, cows fit the bill for domestication very nicely. Domestication of cattle was clearly advantageous to humans, but it also helped the cows. Humans protected the cows from predators and disease, and they cleared the land so that the cows could graze more easily. It was a win-win situation.

However, some scholars disagree with this 7 account that cows were ideal candidates for domestication. They cite recent investigations of the genes of modern cattle, which point to a startling[4] finding. All of today's approximately 1.3 billion cows can be traced back to a herd of about 80 cows that lived somewhere in present-day Iraq or Turkey. This finding suggests that wild cattle were actually very difficult to domesticate. If the process had been easy, it is likely that there would have been a much larger and more diverse gene pool[5] in today's population. These scholars believe that most attempts at domestication were probably not successful. As a result, only the genes of perhaps a single successful attempt are present in today's cattle population.

Domestication of cattle may well have been 8 rare. Yet, today, the more than 800 different breeds of cows suggest that the domestication of cattle has been wildly successful for the Maasai of East Africa and for the rest of the world.

---

[5] *gene pool:* all of the genetic information available for a population

DRINK YOUR MILK!

Historical evidence suggests that early herders were more likely to eat their cows than drink their milk. At that time, most people could not digest cows' milk. It made them sick. But the few people who were able to digest it became strong and healthy. Their babies often survived because they drank cows' milk, which is full of protein, fat, and vitamins. In addition, humans who were able to digest milk produced more children than those who could not and, as a result, passed on their genes for milk digestion.

---

[3] *flight response:* the tendency for an animal to run away when it senses danger

[4] *startling:* very surprising

READING COMPREHENSION

Big Picture

(A) Choose the best answer for each of the following questions.

1. What is the purpose of paragraph 1?
   a. To show that cattle are important in developing countries
   b. To show how cattle lived a long time ago
   c. To illustrate the importance of cattle to an ethnic group

2. Where is the main idea of paragraph 3?
   a. In the first sentence
   b. In the second sentence
   c. In the last sentence

3. What is the main idea of paragraph 6?
   a. Humans benefited from the domestication of cattle.
   b. Cattle were a good candidate for domestication.
   c. Cattle were protected as a result of their domestication.

4. What is the purpose of paragraph 7?
   a. To provide an alternative explanation
   b. To illustrate the success of domestication
   c. To show the scientific foundation of domestication

5. Why do you think the author included the short extra reading, "Drink Your Milk!," on page 98?
   a. To show that humans did not always drink milk
   b. To show the importance of genetics in domestication
   c. To provide more evidence of the importance of cattle in human development

(B) Write a sentence that expresses the main idea of the *whole* reading.

Close-Up

(A) Choose the answer that best completes each of the following sentences. If both choices are correct, circle both.

1. A large herd improves a Maasai man's marriage prospects because _____.
   a. cattle are needed for a wedding   b. cattle indicate wealth

2. According to historians, _____ is a very important development in human history.
   a. the birth of agriculture   b. the domestication of animals

3. Early herders used the skin of their cattle to _____.
   a. build homes   b. make weapons

4. Today, humans probably use the _____ of cows less than early herders did.
   a. bones   b. skin

5. Domestication of cows started _____.
   a. 8,000–10,000 years ago   b. several generations ago

6. An animal that _____ is ideal for domestication.
   a. can accept a human as a leader   b. lives in a herd

7. Long ago, humans helped their cattle by _____.

    a. giving them shelter   **b.** providing an accessible source of food

8. An alternative account of the domestication of cattle suggests that domestication _____.

    a. was rarely successful   **b.** created a diverse gene pool

9. The first domesticated cows were probably from _____.

    a. Turkey or present-day Iraq   **b.** East Africa

10. According to "Drink Your Milk!," the ability to digest milk improved humans' chances of survival because _____.

    a. they did not want to kill their cows   **b.** milk is an excellent source of protein and energy

B Compare answers to Exercise A with a partner. Explain your answers.

Reading Skill

Inferring Meaning from the Text

Not all information in a text is stated directly. Sometimes readers have to *infer* meaning, that is, they have to draw a conclusion based on available information. For example, if you are waiting for a friend and you get a text message that says, "Traffic is terrible," you can infer that your friend will be late. Perhaps, you can even infer that an accident or road construction has caused the delay. Your friend did not provide this information directly; rather, you had to infer it. Making inferences is an important part of careful reading and it will improve your overall comprehension of the text.

A Work with a partner. Read each statement from Reading 1 and "Drink Your Milk!" and answer the questions that follow. The first one is done for you.

1. *Based on archaeological evidence, such as bones and art, scholars believe that the domestication of cattle began between 8,000 and 10,000 years ago.*

How could art provide information about the date of domestication? Describe what that evidence might be.

   Some ancient walls and caves have paintings and drawings that show humans living with cows.

2. *If animals display any of these characteristics, they are unlikely to become domesticated:*

   • *They have a flight response.*

   • *They grow very slowly.*

   • *They cannot breed in captivity.*

   • *They have very specific, inflexible requirements for food and living conditions.*

   • *They are very aggressive or likely to attack.*

The reading does not state directly why these features would make domestication difficult. Choose three of these features and explain why you think each one might make domestication difficult.

   a. _____

   b. _____

   c. _____

3. *They cite recent investigations of the genes of modern cattle, which point to a startling finding. All of today's approximately 1.3 billion cows can be traced back to a herd of about 80 cows that lived somewhere in present-day Iraq or Turkey.*

The reading says this was a startling finding. Why was it startling? What can you infer that the scholars expected to find instead? Why?

_____

4. *At that time, most people could not digest cows' milk.*

Yet today, a significant percentage of the world's population is able to digest cows' milk. Make an inference about why more people can drink milk now than when cows were first domesticated.

_____

B Reread paragraph 6 and think of another inference you can make. Explain it to your partner.

VOCABULARY PRACTICE

Academic Vocabulary

A Find the words in bold in Reading 1. Use the context to help you choose the definition that is closest to the meaning in the reading.

1. prosperity (Par. 1)
   a. health
   b. wealth and good fortune

2. acknowledge (Par. 2)
   a. accept as true
   b. be certain

3. transformation (Par. 2)
   a. long distance
   b. complete change

4. shift (Par. 4)
   a. a change
   b. an increase in importance

5. captivity (Par. 5)
   a. being kept enclosed; imprisoned
   b. being in a herd

6. inflexible (Par. 5)
   a. unable to change
   b. difficult to understand

7. aggressive (Par. 5)
   a. acting shy and unfriendly
   b. acting in an forceful or even angry way

8. advantageous (Par. 6)
   a. beneficial
   b. important

B The words in bold show the academic words from Exercise A and words they often appear with. Complete the sentences with your own ideas.

1. He finally had to **acknowledge that** he would never _____ .

2. _____ **in captivity**, for example, in zoos.

3. The warm weather has been **highly advantageous** for _____ .

4. This wonderful period of **economic prosperity** _____ .

5. With the popularity of cell phones, there has been a **major shift** in how _____ .

6. As a result of the dog's **aggressive behavior**, we _____ .

7. My **schedule** is **totally inflexible**, so I _____ .

8. _____ has **undergone a complete transformation**. I hardly recognize it.

Multiword Vocabulary

(A) Find the words in bold in Reading 1. Then write the words that come before and/or after them to complete the multiword vocabulary.

1. a source of _____ (Par. 1)

2. _____ **back to** (Par. 2)

3. _____ **the way** _____ (Par. 2)

4. rule _____ (Par. 5)

5. living _____ (Par. 5)

6. _____ **the presence** _____ (Par. 6)

7. fit _____ _____ (Par. 6)

8. a _____ **situation** (Par. 6)

(B) Complete the following sentences with the correct multiword vocabulary from Exercise A. Use the information in parentheses to help you. In some cases, you need to change the verb form.

1. If you are looking for an exciting place for a vacation, Las Vegas _____ (is a suitable choice).

2. Concerns about the patient's health _____ (prevent something from happening) the possibility of surgery.

3. After they won the gold medal, the basketball team became _____ (reason to be pleased) for everyone in the country.

4. The _____ (physical environment) for the animals in the zoo were terrible. Their cages were very small and extremely dirty.

5. The agreement between the workers and the company has resulted in _____ (an arrangement that is good for both sides).

6. The museum has a collection of watches that _____ (were made starting in) the 16th century.

7. He made the statement _____ (while they were standing nearby) two police officers.

8. Women such as Indira Gandhi _____ (made it easier for) the women leaders of today.

Use the Vocabulary

Write answers to the following questions. Use the words in bold in your answers. Then share your answers with a partner.

1. Some groups think that animals should not be kept **in captivity** as pets or attractions in zoos. Others think it is **a win-win situation**, **advantageous** for both humans and animals. What is your view?

2. In some communities, people like to watch animals such as crickets, dogs, and chickens fight. **Aggressive** animals are highly valued in these fights. In other communities, this activity is against the law. What is your view of having animals fight for human entertainment?

3. In the past, animals played a vital role in human lives and **prosperity**. This role has **undergone a transformation** and, today, we often view animals as companions rather than workers. What would you say are the causes of this **major shift**?

4. Consider the variety of animals that are kept as pets. If you had to describe the perfect pet, which animal would **fit the bill**?

THINK AND DISCUSS

Work in a small group. Use the information in the reading and your own ideas to discuss the following questions.

1. **Apply knowledge.** Imagine that you are living thousands of years ago. Your food comes from hunting or wild plants that you gather. How do you get the idea to domesticate wild cows?

2. **Evaluate.** Do you agree with the scholars who claim that of all domesticated animals, cattle have been the most important? Do you think another animal has been more important? Explain your answer.

3. **Analyze.** In what ways do you think cows have changed since they were domesticated? Do you think they could become wild again? Explain your answer.

4. **Apply knowledge.** What other wild animals would be suitable for domestication? What features or behaviors make them good candidates?

Are foxes too wild to tame?
Meet the foxes of Novosibirsk,
participants in an experiment
that has continued for more
than fifty years.

READING 2

Academic Vocabulary

to accelerate	docile	solely
affectionate	offspring	a trait
to compress	potential	

Multiword Vocabulary

at work	in close proximity to
to bond with	in the wild
down the road	tone of voice
to hand over	to turn out to be

Reading Preview

Ⓐ Preview. Read the first sentence of each paragraph in Reading 2. Then discuss the following questions with a partner or in a small group.

1. Are foxes wild animals?

2. What kind of experiment does the reading describe?

3. What types of changes happen in animals when they become domesticated?

Ⓑ Topic vocabulary. The following words appear in Reading 2. Look at the words and answer the questions with a partner.

behavior	experiment	hypothesized
breeding	foxes	selective
cages	generation	species
contact	genes	wild

1. Which words are most closely related to animals?

2. Which words might be related to the process of domestication?

3. Which words are used to talk about scientific research?

Ⓒ Predict. What do you think this reading will be about? Discuss each word in Exercise B and predict how it may relate to the reading.

104 UNIT FIVE *Animal–Human Relationships*

Taming the Wild

Cowboys working for the Bureau of Land Management herd wild horses in Winnemucca, Nevada, USA. Many of these wild horses are bought—and tamed—by private citizens.

TAMING THE WILD

"Hello! How are you doing?" Lyudmila 1 Trut asks, looking into the cage labeled "Mavrik." We are on a farm just outside the city of Novosibirsk, in southern Siberia. Although I don't speak Russian, I recognize the affectionate tone of voice that dog owners use with their pets.

Mavrik wags his tail and rolls on his back. 2 He is hoping Trut will pay attention to him. In other cages, there are dozens of other animals doing the same thing. "As you can see," Trut says above the noise, "all of them want human contact." Trut reaches in and scoops Mavrik up, and then hands him over to me. Cradled in my arms, he's as docile as a lapdog.[1] Except that Mavrik is not a dog at all. He's a fox. His behavior is the product of one of the most extraordinary breeding experiments ever conducted.

---

[1] *lapdog:* a small, obedient dog that may be easily held in one's lap

A woman holds a tamed fox on her shoulder.

Some individual wild animals can be tamed and learn to live with humans. This occurs when humans capture a wild animal—a fox, or even a tiger—when it is very young. The animal can be trained to live peacefully in a human environment. However, the tamed animal's offspring will be just as wild as its ancestors. Domestication, in contrast, affects an entire population. It is a process that occurs through many generations, in which wild animals gradually become comfortable living in close proximity to humans. The silver foxes in the Siberian study are truly domesticated, not just tamed.

It all started in 1959, when Trut was still a graduate student. Led by a biologist named Dmitry Belyaev, researchers gathered up 130 foxes from fur farms and began a program of selective breeding. Their goal was to recreate a process similar to the transformation of wolves into dogs, a process that took thousands of years.

In this program, Belyaev and his colleagues first tested each fox's reaction to human contact. Then they selected the most docile ones to breed for the next generation. They continued this process generation after generation. It is important to note that these foxes did not have sustained human contact. The researchers did not attempt to tame them. Belyaev wanted to be sure that any changes in the foxes' behavior were the result of selective breeding rather than training. By the mid-1960s the researchers were achieving great success. They were producing foxes that were not only unafraid of humans but that were also eager to bond with them. Miraculously, the researchers had accelerated domestication solely through selective breeding. They had compressed a process that usually takes thousands of years into just a few generations.

Belyaev wasn't just trying to create friendly foxes, however. He wanted to unlock the secrets of domestication. Domesticated animals are known to share a set of similar physical characteristics. They tend to be smaller than their wild counterparts, with floppy ears and curly tails. They often have spotted coats instead of the solid coats that are more common in the wild. These changes tend to make the animals look like juveniles,[2] which are more attractive to humans. In short, domesticated animals are cuter than their wild ancestors. These traits exist, to varying degrees, across a remarkably wide range of species that have been domesticated, from dogs and pigs to cows and chickens.

"Their goal was to recreate a process similar to the transformation of wolves into dogs, a process that took thousands of years."

When the experiment began in 1959, Belyaev predicted that as his foxes became domesticated, they too might begin to show some of these physical traits. His prediction turned out to be correct. Breeding foxes based solely on their behavior resulted in changes in their physical appearance. After only nine generations, the foxes had developed floppier ears, and spots began to appear on their coats. The foxes were also wagging their tails like dogs in the presence of humans, a clear behavioral sign of domestication.

Belyaev hypothesized that a collection of genes was responsible for these physical and behavioral traits. He believed that his domesticated foxes shared them with other domesticated species. He proposed that in the history of domestication, these animals had experienced specific changes in their genes. These changes caused them to be less afraid of humans and, thus, willing to live closer to them. Perhaps they ate food that humans left, or perhaps living near humans offered them protection from predators. At some point, however, early humans realized the potential benefit of these animal neighbors and began helping the process of domestication along. Humans actively selected the friendliest ones and began to breed them. "At the beginning of the domestication process, only natural selection[3] was at work," as Trut puts it. "Down the road, this natural selection was replaced with artificial selection."

---

[2] *juveniles:* young animals or people

[3] *natural selection:* a process in which only those plants and animals with characteristics that allow them to live successfully in a particular environment are likely to live and reproduce

READING COMPREHENSION

Big Picture

A The following statements are the main ideas of some of the paragraphs in Reading 2. Write the correct paragraph number next to its main idea.

_____ **1.** In a scientific experiment, researchers were able to significantly speed up the domestication process.

_____ **2.** There is probably a genetic explanation for domestication.

_____ **3.** Many domestic animals display similar physical features and behavior.

_____ **4.** Taming and domestication are quite different processes.

_____ **5.** The silver foxes developed the physical features that come with domestication.

B Read the following statements. Check (✓) the statement that expresses the main idea of the *whole* reading.

_____ **1.** Selective breeding is more effective than natural selection.

_____ **2.** Physical, behavioral, and genetic traits accompany domestication.

_____ **3.** Selective breeding is an important scientific tool.

_____ **4.** Domestic animals are fundamentally different from their wild counterparts.

Close-Up

A Decide which of the following statements are true or false according to the reading. Write *T* (True) or *F* (False) next to each one.

_____ **1.** The foxes in the cages seem very friendly.

_____ **2.** Tame animals can peacefully live among humans.

_____ **3.** Tame animals usually have tame babies.

_____ **4.** It is possible to domesticate an individual animal.

_____ **5.** In the beginning of the experiment, the foxes spent a lot of time with humans.

_____ **6.** The domestication of the foxes occurred relatively quickly.

_____ **7.** Wild animals usually have floppy ears and curly tails.

_____ **8.** Tail wagging is a form of behavior that comes with domestication.

_____ **9.** Belyaev found the gene responsible for domestication.

_____ **10.** According to the scientists in the reading, domestication has included both natural and selective breeding.

B Work with a partner or in a small group. Change the false statements in Exercise A to make them true.

Reading Skill

A In Reading 2, underline the sentences that describe the two processes: *domestication* and *selective breeding*. Then answer the questions.

	Domestication Evidence from the Reading	Selective Breeding Evidence from the Reading
1. Does the author give a definition?		
2. Does the author describe the steps in the process?		
3. What is the process contrasted with?		

B Compare answers to Exercise A with a partner. Discuss any differences in your answers.

VOCABULARY PRACTICE

Academic Vocabulary

A Find the words in bold in Reading 2. Use the context and the sentences below to help you choose the correct definition.

1. Children are often very **affectionate** (Par. 1) with their grandparents. They give them hugs and kisses.
   - **a.** showing loving behavior
   - **b.** dependent

2. The horse was very **docile** (Par. 2). He ate carrots from the child's hand and let her pet him.
   - **a.** strong
   - **b.** easy to control

3. A mother lion looks after her **offspring** (Par. 3) for about two years after they are born.
   - **a.** prey
   - **b.** babies

4. Laptops and cell phones have **accelerated** (Par. 5) the shift to digital communication.
   - **a.** made faster
   - **b.** made more efficient

5. Admission to the university is based **solely** (Par. 5) on a student's test scores.
   - **a.** only
   - **b.** partly

6. Everyone is very busy, so we have **compressed** (Par. 5) all of our business into one day.

    a. pushed something big into a small space or time   **b.** finished quickly

7. Twins share many physical **traits** (Par. 6).

    a. characteristics   **b.** structures

8. Unfortunately, there are many **potential** (Par. 8) problems with the new school plan.

    a. unfamiliar to most people   **b.** possible; likely to develop

B Read the following sentences and circle the correct word to complete each one. The correct word is frequently used with the word in bold; the other is not.

1. The promising new drug offers **potential** (benefits / injury) for patients with many types of cancer.

2. Many mammals (produce / keep) **offspring** only once every two or three years.

3. Children often (exhibit / prefer) physical and personality **traits** that are similar to those of their parents.

4. In some cultures, **affectionate** (emotion / behavior) in public is not acceptable.

5. After an injury, heat can **accelerate** the (process / possibility) of healing.

6. The computer program can **compress** a great deal of information (for / into) a small space.

Multiword Vocabulary

A Find the words in bold in Reading 2. Then use the words from the box below to complete the multiword vocabulary.

bond	hands	proximity	road	turned	voice	wild	work

1. tone of _____ (Par. 1)

2. _____ him **over** (Par. 2)

3. in close _____ **to** (Par. 3)

4. _____ **with** (Par. 5)

5. in the _____ (Par. 6)

6. _____ **out to be** (Par. 7)

7. at _____ (Par. 8)

8. down the _____ (Par. 8)

B Complete the following sentences with the correct multiword vocabulary from Exercise A. Use the information in parentheses to help you. In some cases, you may need to change the verb form.

1. Whenever the baby starts to cry, the grandmother _____ (give him) to his mother.

2. The hotel is _____ (near) all of the tourist attractions, so we will not have to walk very far.

3. Baby animals _____ (in a natural state, without humans) look cute, but they are still dangerous.

4. Scientists are trying to understand the forces _____ (that have an influence or control) inside a volcano.

5. It's too early to think about next year's budget. We will worry about it
_____ (later; in the future).

6. We liked our new neighbor, so we were surprised when he _____
(was discovered to be) a criminal.

7. The receptionist could tell that the caller was angry by her _____
(the way people sound when they speak).

8. Most children _____ (develop a close connection to) their
parents soon after they are born.

Use the Vocabulary

Write answers to the following questions. Use the words in bold in your answers. Then
share your answers with a partner.

1. What **traits** do you think are important in a pet? Do you prefer pets that are **affectionate** and
docile? Or, do you like pets that are playful and have a lot of energy? Explain your preference.

2. Have you ever had the experience of liking someone when you first meet him or her and
then, **down the road**, he or she **turns out to be** a completely different person? Describe
your experience.

3. What can you learn about a person's mood based **solely** on **tone of voice**?

4. Would you like to live far away from or **in close proximity to** your job? Do you think there are
potential problems with living close to your work?

THINK AND DISCUSS

Work in a small group. Use the information in the reading and your own ideas to
discuss the following questions.

1. **Evaluate.** Do you think that the silver-fox experiment has been important? Explain
your answer.

2. **Predict.** How might the results of the experiment help animals or humans in the future?

3. **Make an inference.** The silver-fox experiment has been going on for more than 50 years. Why
do you think it has lasted for this long?

4. **Express an opinion.** Do you think experiments such as this one are cruel, that is, unkind to
the animals?

5. **Relate to personal experience.** Would you like to have a silver fox as a pet? What do you think
it would be like?

Vocabulary Review

A Complete the reading with the vocabulary below that you have studied in the unit.

accelerate the process	bond with	in the presence of	undergo a complete transformation
acknowledged that	dates back to	potential benefit	win-win situation
affectionate behavior	down the road		

Meet Vi, a dog that lives in a home for children who are getting treatment at a nearby hospital. The young patients quickly _____ her because of her sweet and

_____ . She lets them pat her head and scratch her belly. However, Vi does
     2

more than just bring smiles to the children. She also provides a(n) _____ for
                                                                 3

the children's health. This idea of pet therapy _____ the 18th century, when it
                             4

was discovered that pets helped people relax. Researchers have found that patients' stress levels

and blood pressure often go down _____ friendly animals. These changes can
                                                    5

_____ of healing—for example, after a heart attack or serious surgery—
      6

perhaps more efficiently and safely than some drugs. It is possible that _____ ,
                                                                            7

pet therapy will become a common future treatment option.

In the past, pet therapy focused on patients and how animals could help them to recover. More

recently, researchers have _____ that the interaction helps the pets, too. For
                                        8

example, some aggressive and disobedient dogs can _____ once they start
                                                               9

working in pet therapy settings. It seems that animal–human interaction is a(n)

_____ for everyone—both dogs and humans.
      10

B Compare answers to Exercise A with a partner. Then discuss the following questions.

Do you think pet therapy would help you get better if you were sick? How?

C Complete the following sentences in a way that shows that you understand the meaning of the words in bold.

1. I prefer pets that **exhibit traits** such as _____ .

2. There has been a **major shift** in _____ .

3. I live **in close proximity to** _____ .

4. _____ is **a source of pride** for _____ .

D Work with a partner and write sentences that include any six of the vocabulary items below. You may use any verb tense and make nouns plural if you wish.

at work	fit the bill	in captivity	rule out
based solely	hand over	pave the way for	turn out to be
economic prosperity	highly advantageous		

Connect the Readings

A With a partner, study the photos below of wild animals and their domesticated counterparts. How are the pairs different? For each pair, write a sentence describing the physical characteristics that have changed in the domesticated animal.

Wild Animals	Domesticated Animals
 Gray wolf	 Dog
 Wild sheep	 Sheep
 Cougar	 Cat

1. _____

2. _____

3. _____

B With a partner or in a small group, compare your answers to Exercise A. Then discuss which animal you think has changed the most.

C Discuss the following questions with a partner. Use your understanding of the readings and your own ideas.

1. How has the animal you chose in Exercise B changed the lives of humans?
2. How has domestication changed the life of this animal?

A laser show lights up
Marina Bay, Singapore.

FOCUS

1. How do the buildings you live and work in affect the way you feel?

2. How do these buildings reflect the culture of the communities where they are located?

Architecture

Academic Vocabulary

brittle	innovative	a safeguard
discouraging	an occupant	to withstand
elaborate	resilient	

Multiword Vocabulary

to be prone to	a matter of life and
beyond one's	death
means	to not stand a chance of
death toll	to pay off
a fact of life	to say nothing of

Reading Preview

A **Preview.** Look at Figures 1 and 2 and Tables 1 and 2 on pages 118–120. Then discuss the following questions with a partner or in a small group.

1. What building materials in Figure 1 do you think are the safest?

2. Which parts of the world have experienced the most earthquakes?

3. In which countries have the most people died as a result of earthquakes?

B **Topic vocabulary.** The following words appear in Reading 1. Look at the words and answer the questions with a partner.

brick	earthquakes	shock
collapse	engineers	straw
concrete	fatalities	tremors
construction	shaking	tumbling

1. Which words are most closely related to building?

2. Which words are about danger and destruction?

3. Which words describe movement?

C **Predict.** What do you think this reading will be about? Discuss each word in Exercise B and predict how it may relate to the reading.

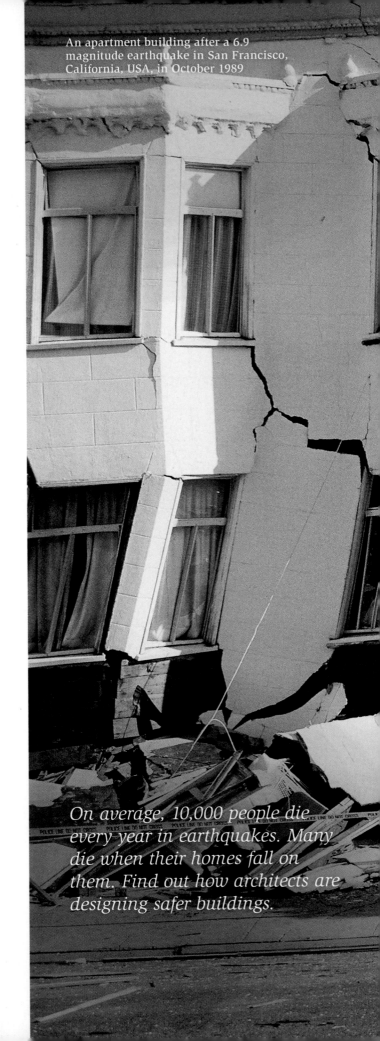

An apartment building after a 6.9 magnitude earthquake in San Francisco, California, USA, in October 1989

On average, 10,000 people die every year in earthquakes. Many die when their homes fall on them. Find out how architects are designing safer buildings.

Safer Homes in Earthquake Zones

One engineer sums it up in a few brief words: "Earthquakes don't kill; buildings do." In Los Angeles, Tokyo, and other wealthy cities in earthquake zones, high-tech, earthquake-resistant construction has become an expensive fact of life. Engineers reinforce concrete walls with steel. Some recent buildings rest on elaborate shock absorbers that have many layers of padding. Experts say these kinds of safeguards have paid off. They believe that strict building codes[1] saved thousands of lives when an earthquake hit Chile in 2010. It was the sixth most powerful earthquake on record. There was extensive damage. Yet, the death toll—521—was relatively low.

People in less developed countries have not been so lucky, however. Haiti also experienced a strong earthquake in 2010. Although the one in Chile was 500 times more powerful, the Haitian quake killed at least 223,000 people and left more than a million homeless (see Tables 1 and 2). In Haiti and other countries with few resources, expensive, earthquake-resistant structures don't stand a chance of getting built. Even basic earthquake engineering is often beyond their means. Billions of people live in houses that can't withstand the violent shaking of an earthquake. Fortunately, safer homes can be built cheaply, using local material such as straw, bamboo,[2] and recycled materials like old tires.

---

[1] *building codes:* government rules for safe construction

[2] *bamboo:* a tropical grass with hard, hollow stems

Figure 1. Inexpensive Earthquake-Resistant Construction

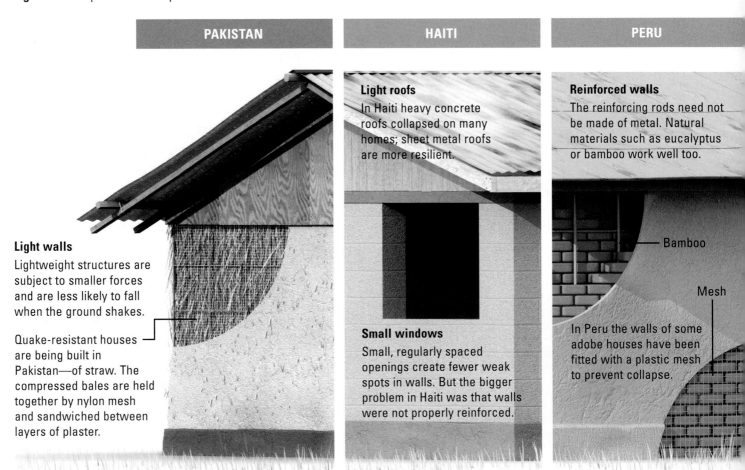

PAKISTAN

Light walls
Lightweight structures are subject to smaller forces and are less likely to fall when the ground shakes.

Quake-resistant houses are being built in Pakistan—of straw. The compressed bales are held together by nylon mesh and sandwiched between layers of plaster.

HAITI

Light roofs
In Haiti heavy concrete roofs collapsed on many homes; sheet metal roofs are more resilient.

Small windows
Small, regularly spaced openings create fewer weak spots in walls. But the bigger problem in Haiti was that walls were not properly reinforced.

PERU

Reinforced walls
The reinforcing rods need not be made of metal. Natural materials such as eucalyptus or bamboo work well too.

Bamboo

Mesh

In Peru the walls of some adobe houses have been fitted with a plastic mesh to prevent collapse.

Source: National Geographic Magazine, June 2010

Table 1. Earthquakes with Highest Death Tolls since 1900

Country	Date	Magnitude	Fatalities
China	1976	7.0	242,000
Haiti	2010	7.0	223,000
China	1920	7.8	180,000
Indonesia	2004	9.1	165,000*
Japan	1923	7.9	143,000
Soviet Union (present day Turkmenistan)	1948	7.3	110,000
Italy	1908	7.1	75,000
Pakistan	2005	7.6	73,000
China	2008	7.9	69,000

*includes deaths from tsunami caused by earthquake
Source: EM-DAT, Centre for Research on the Epidemiology of Disasters

Table 2. Earthquakes with Highest Magnitudes since 1900

Country	Date	Magnitude	Fatalities
Chile	1960	9.5	1,655
Alaska, USA	1964	9.2	128
Indonesia	2004	9.1	165,000*
Japan	2011	9.0	16,000
Kamchatka, Soviet Union	1952	9.0	0
Chile	2010	8.8	521
off coast of Ecuador	1906	8.8	500–1,500
Alaska, USA	1965	8.7	0
Indonesia	2005	8.6	1,300

*includes deaths from tsunami caused by earthquake
Source: Australia Geographic

INDONESIA

Shock absorbers
Tires filled with stones or sand and fastened between floor and foundation can serve as cheap shock absorbers for many types of building.

"The devastation in Haiti wouldn't happen in a developed country," says engineer Marcial Blondet of the Catholic University of Peru. Blondet has been working on innovative building ideas since 1970, when an earthquake in Peru killed 70,000 people. Many of the victims died when their houses crumbled around them. Heavy, brittle walls of traditional sundried brick cracked instantly when the ground started shaking. Subsequent tremors brought roofs tumbling down. Blondet's research team has found that brick walls like these can be reinforced with a strong plastic mesh.[3] In an earthquake, walls will crack, but they won't collapse. The occupants may lose their homes, but they won't lose their lives. This inexpensive plastic mesh can also reinforce concrete walls like the ones that are common in Haiti.

Engineers in other countries are also working on methods that use other types of inexpensive and local materials. Researchers in India have successfully tested concrete house walls reinforced with bamboo, which is both cheap and

[3] *mesh:* loosely woven material with big spaces, much like a net

Figure 2. Map of Seismic Activity around the World

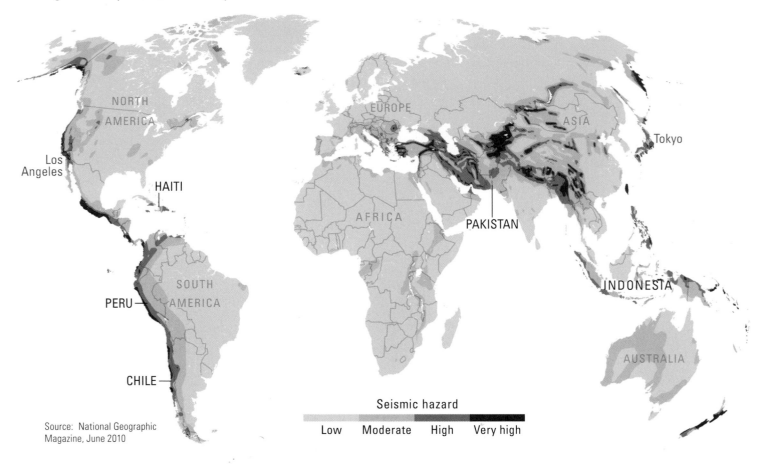

Seismic hazard

Low   Moderate   High   Very high

Source: National Geographic
Magazine, June 2010

widely available there. In Indonesia, a model house rests on a foundation of old tires filled with sand. These kinds of houses are not as strong as houses that use more sophisticated earthquake-resistant technology, but they cost much less. The lower cost means they are more likely to be built in countries like Indonesia.

John van de Lindt, a professor 5 of civil engineering at Colorado State University, knows that choosing the right building materials can be a matter of life and death in an earthquake zone. He says that builders and engineers want buildings to be as safe as possible. Yet, they must also be realistic about costs. Working with local materials is an important first step. In northern Pakistan, this means straw. Traditional houses are built of stone and mud, but straw is far

"John van de Lindt… knows that choosing the right building materials can be a matter of life and death in an earthquake zone."

more resilient during earthquakes, according to California engineer Darcey Donovan. She and her colleagues started building straw houses in Pakistan after the 2005 earthquake.

There are similar challenges 6 in other areas that are prone to earthquakes. There are many exciting ideas, but the slow progress is discouraging. One major problem is that even these cheap solutions aren't always cheap enough. Since 2007, only about 2,500 houses in Peru have been reinforced with plastic mesh. Unfortunately, that still leaves millions of unsafe houses in Peru, to say nothing of other developing countries. Blondet acknowledges that many houses will collapse in the next earthquake. Fortunately, however, there are also many more safe houses made of local materials that are likely to withstand future earthquakes.

READING COMPREHENSION

Big Picture

A Choose the best answer for each of the following questions.

1. What is the main idea of paragraph 1?
   a. Many countries cannot afford to build earthquake-resistant homes.
   b. The number of deaths from earthquakes is very high.
   c. Earthquake-resistant construction can save lives.

2. What is the purpose of paragraphs 3, 4, and 5?
   a. To show that engineers are helping communities that have experienced earthquakes
   b. To show that local and inexpensive building materials can be earthquake resistant
   c. To show the high-tech innovations in earthquake-resistant construction

3. The following sentence is the main idea for which paragraph?

   Although there are inexpensive ways to construct earthquake-resistant buildings, for some communities, these are still too expensive.

   a. Paragraph 4
   b. Paragraph 5
   c. Paragraph 6

4. What is the main idea of Reading 1?
   a. Earthquake-resistant construction is too expensive for some countries.
   b. Inexpensive earthquake-resistant construction is possible.
   c. More people will die in earthquakes if we don't build better houses.

B In Exercise A, question 2 suggests that paragraphs 3, 4, and 5 all have similar purposes. Write the main idea of each paragraph.

1. Paragraph 3: _____

2. Paragraph 4: _____

3. Paragraph 5: _____

Close-Up

A Briefly answer the following questions according to information in Reading 1.

1. Why was the earthquake damage so much worse in Haiti than in Chile?

   _____

2. How can plastic mesh help save lives?

   _____

3. What are the advantages of building materials such as bamboo and old tires?

   _____

4. Why is straw a good building material for areas that experience a lot of earthquakes?

   _____

5. Why aren't more communities adopting the new building ideas described in the reading?

B Briefly answer the following question after studying Figure 1.

What are two building suggestions shown in Figure 1 that are not discussed in the reading?

Reading Skill

Understanding Information in Tables

Academic texts often include tables and graphs. These visuals may show information in the main text in a different form, or they may provide additional information. It is important to understand how the tables are connected to the main text.

1. Look for references to tables and graphs within the text (for example, *see Tables 1 and 2*). The surrounding text probably contains information closely connected to the information in the table.

2. Think about how the information in tables and graphs extends the ideas and arguments presented in the text.

A Look at Tables 1 and 2. Work with a partner to answer the following questions.

1. What information in the reading is also in the tables? Underline the overlapping information in the tables and the text.

2. For the events or ideas that you underlined in the reading, what additional information does the table provide?

B Compare the information in the two tables. Then discuss the following questions with a partner.

1. There were two earthquakes in the former Soviet Union only four years apart. Which earthquake had more fatalities? Why do you think the number of fatalities was so different?

2. Why do you think two of the most powerful earthquakes in the tables had no fatalities?

3. Which earthquake is listed in both Table 1 and Table 2? Why do you think only one earthquake is found in both tables?

4. What factors could explain the number of fatalities in both tables?

5. Based on the information in the tables, where do you think another major earthquake might occur in the future? Where do you think an earthquake with a high number of fatalities might occur? Explain your answers.

VOCABULARY PRACTICE

Academic Vocabulary

A Find the words in bold in Reading 1. Use the context and the sentences below to help you match each word to its correct definition.

_____ 1. The children spent days creating an **elaborate** (Par. 1) plan for a surprise birthday party.

_____ 2. The new law includes **safeguards** (Par. 1) against dangerous chemicals.

_____ 3. Airplane parts must **withstand** (Par. 2) the force of high winds and changes in temperature.

_____ 4. The engineers used **innovative** (Par. 3) methods to build the bridge.

_____ 5. Because their bones are **brittle** (Par. 3), it can be quite serious when old people fall.

_____ 6. All of the **occupants** (Par. 3) of the apartment building were able to escape the fire.

_____ 7. The plants in this area are naturally **resilient** (Par. 5) and grew back quickly after the drought.

_____ 8. The report was very **discouraging** (Par. 6). The police were unable to find the mountain climbers who got lost in the snowstorm.

a. stiff but easily broken

b. not easily harmed or damaged; able to recover

c. people who live inside a place

d. causing a feeling of hopelessness or lack of confidence to continue

e. new, different, and usually better

f. very complicated with many different parts

g. survive without damage

h. methods of protection from harm

B Choose an academic word from Exercise A to complete each of the following sentences. Notice and learn the words in bold because they often appear with the academic words.

1. In spite of the cold winter, the trees we planted last year turned out to be **remarkably** _____. This spring they are growing well.

2. In a special course, the teachers learned to use simple but _____ **ideas** in their classes to help students who struggle with their work.

3. The software engineers have created a(n) _____ **system** that no one understands. It is extremely complicated.

4. The _____ of the **building** say that the elevator needs repairs. Several people have gotten stuck in it.

5. The equipment is used in polar areas because it is able to _____ **extreme temperatures** and remain effective.

6. We were disappointed by the _____ **news** about the economy.

7. Older people often have _____ **bones** that break easily.

8. We must develop _____ **against** future natural disasters.

A collapsed building after the Haiti earthquake in 2010

Multiword Vocabulary

A Find the multiword vocabulary in bold in Reading 1 and use the context to help you figure out the meaning. Then match each item to the correct definition.

_____ **1. a fact of life** (Par. 1)

_____ **2. paid off** (Par. 1)

_____ **3. death toll** (Par. 1)

_____ **4. don't stand a chance of** (Par. 2)

_____ **5. beyond their means** (Par. 2)

_____ **6. a matter of life and death** (Par. 5)

_____ **7. are prone to** (Par. 6)

_____ **8. to say nothing of** (Par. 6)

a. the number of people who have died

b. have the tendency to be affected by something bad

c. extremely important; important enough to affect someone's survival

d. have no possibility of

e. in addition to and even more important than

f. was successful after a period of time

g. something that cannot be changed and must be accepted

h. too expensive for them

B Complete the following sentences using the correct multiword vocabulary from Exercise A. In some cases, you need to change the verb or pronoun form.

1. This has been a terrible winter. The temperatures have been extremely low, _____ the heavy snow.

2. The _____ from this weekend's tragic fire has reached four.

3. We would like to take a vacation this summer, but I am afraid, for now, it is _____. Maybe we will be able to afford it next year.

4. For top mountain climbers, having the right equipment can be _____. Poor preparations can have fatal consequences.

5. Our soccer team is not very strong this year. I am afraid we _____ making it to the championship match.

6. An investment in your education will _____ eventually because it will enable you to get a good job.

7. For people who live in Alaska, long, cold winters are just _____.

8. People who _____ respiratory problems should stay inside today. The pollution is very bad.

Use the Vocabulary

Write answers to the following questions. Use the words in bold in your answers. Then share your answers with a partner.

1. Are you **prone to** catching colds? If so, what are the best **safeguards against** catching them?

2. Some people believe that children are more **resilient** than adults following a serious illness or a tragedy. Do you think this is the case?

3. Have you ever made a plan or done something that others said **didn't stand a chance of** succeeding? Did your plan **pay off** in the end?

4. Most people dream of doing something or buying something that is **beyond their means**. What do you dream about?

5. What do you when you get **discouraging news**? Do you accept it as **a fact of life**? Try to change it? Try to think about other things? Give an example of discouraging news you have heard.

THINK AND DISCUSS

Work in a small group. Use the information in the reading and your own ideas to discuss the following questions.

1. **Summarize.** How would you describe the connection between the magnitude of an earthquake and the number of fatalities it causes?

2. **Analyze.** Reading 1 contains the following statement, "The occupants may lose their homes, but they won't lose their lives." Explain what this means. Should governments in these countries focus on expensive solutions, which may save buildings, or inexpensive solutions, which may not save the buildings themselves but will save the people inside these buildings?

3. **Predict.** How successful do you think the efforts to use inexpensive materials described in Reading 1 will be over time? Explain your answer.

Academic Vocabulary

apparent	to filter	to update
to blend	to incorporate	ventilation
an element	inspiration	

Multiword Vocabulary

at the same time	in keeping with
a breath of fresh air	to keep something in mind
an extended family	to make way for
to get in touch with	turn of the century

Reading Preview

A **Preview.** Look at the photos on pages 126–130 and read their captions. Then discuss the following questions with a partner or in a small group.

1. Which buildings are modern with high-tech architecture? Which buildings have a traditional design?

2. Where do you think these different styles of architecture are popular? Why do you think they are popular?

3. Do the buildings in the photos have anything in common? Explain your answer.

B **Topic vocabulary.** The following words appear in Reading 2. Look at the words and answer the questions with a partner.

breezes	identities	style
design	materials	sunlight
heritage	screens	tile
high-rise	steel	tradition

1. Which words are closely related to building and architecture?

2. Which words are related to nature?

3. What words are used to describe culture?

C **Predict.** What do you think this reading will be about? Discuss each word in Exercise B and predict how it may relate to the reading.

The Absolute World residential towers in Mississauga, Canada

Do traditional designs have a place in our modern world of steel and concrete? Learn how architects in Asia are finding ways to make traditional and modern architecture work together.

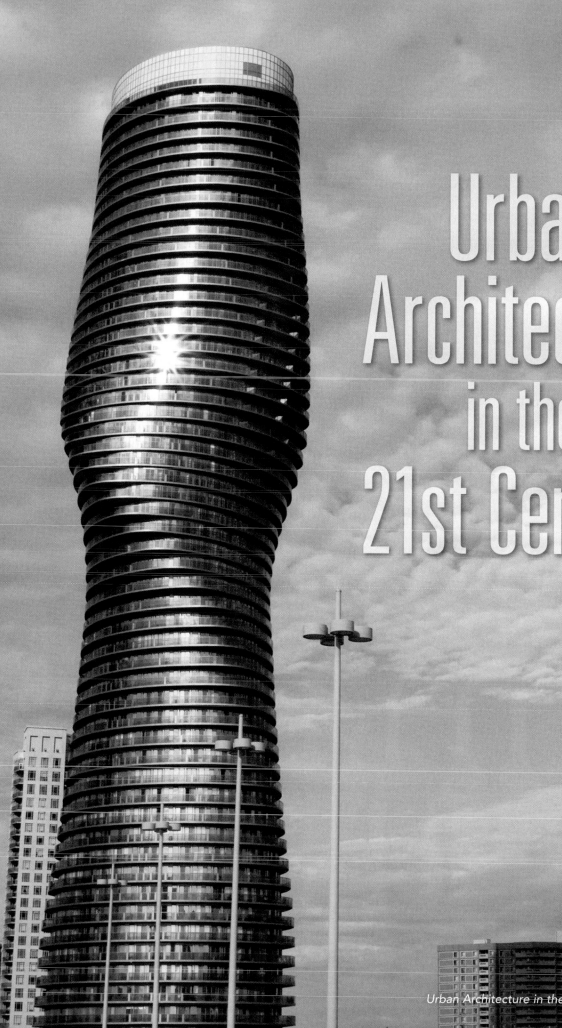

Urban
Architecture
in the
21st Century

The skyscraper—from London to Hong Kong to Toronto—is the standard of a modern, global style. With roots in late 19th-century Chicago, the skyscraper became possible with new building materials and emerging technology: steel beams, reinforced concrete, and the elevator. This architectural style quickly spread around the world. Every growing city wanted to show it was part of the modern world. By the end of the 20th century, many cities had torn down old neighborhoods to make way for modern building projects. As a result, the business centers of many cities around the world began to look alike. They were filled with high-rise office and apartment buildings—tall towers of glass and steel. Houston? Singapore? São Paolo? It became hard to tell them apart.

At the turn of the 21st century, many city residents and architects began to ask themselves questions: Is this how we want our cities to look? In order to be modern, must our cities give up their individual identities? Can elements of local tradition, design, and materials be incorporated into modern architecture?

Modern Style and Local Traditions

Some architects have answered these questions by incorporating traditional design elements into their skyscrapers. For example, the Taipei 101 Building in Taipei and the Jin Mao Tower in Shanghai are basically modern. However, they also include elements of traditional Chinese architecture. Even those who are unfamiliar with Chinese architecture will recognize the features of a pagoda[1] in these two buildings.

The use of traditional architectural features affects more than a building's appearance.

---

[1] *pagoda:* traditional style of religious building in East and Southeast Asia

The Al Bahar Towers, Abu Dhabi, United Arab Emirates

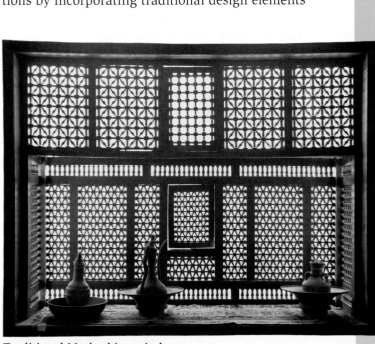
Traditional Mashrabiya window screen

Building designed by Chinese architect, Wang Shu

Traditional design features are often functional. One example is the lattice[2] window of traditional Arab homes—the *mashrabiya*. This type of window permits air and some light to enter the room. At the same time, it protects the room from strong, direct sunlight. It also allows privacy, which is important in traditional Arab culture, especially for women. This idea has been updated with modern technology in the Al Bahar Towers in Abu Dhabi, where the sun can heat windows up to 200 degrees Fahrenheit (90 degrees Celsius). Computer-controlled lattice screens cover the windows of this high-rise building. They fold and unfold in response to the movement of the sun. They keep the building cool but allow in some natural light. This traditional feature has helped reduce the cost of lighting and air-conditioning by almost 50 percent. In addition, it includes local elements in the primarily modern design.

---

[2] *lattice:* a pattern of diagonal strips of wood that leaves openings between the strips

Preserving Local Traditions in Asia

5 Some architects are questioning the dominance of modern design. They are returning to local traditions and, often, local materials. This trend is particularly apparent in Asian countries with strong, emerging economies.

6 In China, internationally acclaimed architect Wang Shu wants to bring a breath of fresh air to modern design. He is creating designs in which modern concrete and Chinese traditional building practices can coexist. Traditional Chinese buildings, including homes, often have outdoor spaces on the inside. Wang says that the most important thing for Chinese people is not the building itself. It is "living in some peaceful place with trees, water, and your family together." He tries to keep this idea in mind when he designs buildings. He reuses old material such as tile and brick in his new buildings. He says that in China, builders have always used materials over and over again. Some buildings may contain materials that come from structures that were

built hundreds of years ago. Wang believes that this is what gives a building its spirit and makes it feel alive.

Vietnamese architect Vo Truong Nghia also looks to the past for inspiration, in this case, the traditional Vietnamese *tube houses*. These tall, narrow houses were once typical in urban areas. They usually had a business on the bottom floor and then living quarters for an extended family on the upper floors. The buildings were open on all sides, allowing in light and cool breezes. Nghia has designed a modern tube house. It has four floors and stands on a lot that is only 13 x 65 feet (3.96 x 19.81 meters). Each floor has one room that is open all around. Instead of curtains, a row of plants on each floor filters the light and maintains the family's privacy. A garden on the roof keeps the whole house cool. This design has become popular with young Vietnamese who want to return to local traditions but enjoy modern comfort.

As in Vietnam, many young professionals in South Korea don't want to live in western-style, high-rise apartments. They want to get in touch with their cultural heritage without giving up modern conveniences. In keeping with these wishes, architect Doojin Hwang has updated the traditional *hanok*. A hanok is a small building—usually a home or small business. It is built with natural materials such as wood, stone, and earth. It has a traditional heating system that sends hot air underneath the floor so the building stays warm in the winter. Its design and natural ventilation keep it cool in the summer without air-conditioning.

Hwang did not start out his career designing traditional homes. At first, he worked on large, modern building projects. He says, "As I grew older, I realized I am a *Korean* architect. . . . Architects have to work within the community." Here and all over Asia, architects and urban residents are finding ways to create new from old, and blend the modern and traditional.

Vietnamese tube houses

READING COMPREHENSION

Big Picture

A Read the following statements. Check (✓) the four statements that express the main ideas of Reading 2.

_____ **1.** Many old buildings don't need air-conditioning.

_____ **2.** Some traditional homes can keep occupants comfortable without a lot of technology.

_____ **3.** Some people like modern buildings, and others like traditional designs.

_____ **4.** Some traditional designs can save energy, even in modern buildings.

_____ **5.** The skyscraper has roots in Chicago.

_____ **6.** Many recent architectural designs combine local traditions with modern ideas.

_____ **7.** Some architects reuse material from older buildings.

_____ **8.** People are beginning to question the destruction of old buildings and their replacement with modern ones.

B Of the four statements you selected in Exercise A, which one best expresses the main idea of the *whole* reading?

Close-Up

A List two benefits of each of the building elements or styles mentioned in Reading 2.

1. *Mashrabiya* windows

_____

_____

2. Modern tube houses

_____

_____

3. Traditional *hanoks*

_____

_____

B Compare answers to Exercise A with a partner. Can you find any of the features in the photos on pages 128, 130, and 132?

Hanok style house,
South Korea

Reading Skill

When you take notes on a reading, you want to capture the main ideas and some of the details that support the main ideas. Underlining or highlighting important points is a good first step, but taking notes can give you a deeper understanding of the material. It also makes it easier to study the information in the reading for a test. When you take notes, don't copy down complete sentences. Just write a few words that will help you remember the most important points in the text. You can make these notes in the margins of the text or in a separate notebook with page references.

1. Write down the main ideas of the text. You may not need one for each paragraph.

2. Write down a few notes that show how the author supported each main idea. The author might have used an example, statistics, or results of a study.

A Read the following paragraph. On the lines below it, write notes that include the main idea and two details that support the paragraph.

Houses made of brick or stone are strong and can withstand strong winds and rain. So, some people had doubts when a group in the Philippines decided to build a school entirely of bamboo. What would happen during a powerful storm? Such storms often pass through the Philippines and damage or destroy buildings. Was it wise to choose a building material that is so weak and flimsy? The builders gave two reasons for their choice. First, bamboo is more resilient than wood or steel. During storms with strong winds, bamboo walls may sway and bend, but they don't often break. As a result, bamboo structures may actually survive storms more successfully than structures built from stronger, more rigid materials. Second, if some pieces of the bamboo structure are damaged, they can be replaced easily. Forests of bamboo grow in close proximity to the school. If parts of the school have to be rebuilt after a storm, the raw materials are inexpensive and readily available.

Main idea: _____

   Supporting details:

   _____

   _____

B Review these main idea statements from Big Picture, Exercise A. Then, for each one, write one or two supporting details.

1. People are beginning to question the destruction of old buildings and their replacement with modern ones.

Supporting detail(s):

_____

_____

2. Many recent architectural designs combine local traditions with modern ideas.

Supporting detail(s):

_____

_____

VOCABULARY PRACTICE

Academic Vocabulary

A Find the words in bold in Reading 2. Use the context and the sentences below to help you match each word to its correct definition.

_____ **1.** The museum exhibit included **elements** (Par. 2) of the different cultures of Mexico.

_____ **2.** My business professor **incorporated** (Par. 2) what he learned as a banker into our course.

_____ **3.** The hotel **updated** (Par. 4) its rooms with new furniture and curtains.

_____ **4.** It was **apparent** (Par. 5) from her tone of voice that she was displeased.

_____ **5.** Artists find their **inspiration** (Par. 7) in unexpected places.

_____ **6.** The big tree outside my window **filters** (Par. 7) most of the sound from the outside, so my room is very quiet.

_____ **7.** The **ventilation** (Par. 8) is not very good in my office, so it feels very uncomfortable in the afternoons.

_____ **8.** Her novels **blend** (Par. 9) the past, present, and future, making them difficult to follow.

a. reduces something by allowing only part of it through

b. parts or features of a larger unit or system

c. included something as part of something larger

d. the movement of fresh air through a room or building

e. made something more modern

f. easy to see or understand

g. mix or combine

h. someone or something that gives you new and creative ideas

B Choose an academic word from Exercise A to complete each of the following sentences. Notice and learn the words in bold because they often appear with the academic words. In some cases, you need to change the verb form.

1. The chef _____ **together** the traditional flavors of China, India, and Malaysia to create the taste of Singapore.

2. A **key** _____ of the economic plan is an increase in taxes.

3. Painters in the early 20th century **drew** _____ **from** the natural world.

4. The unique design of the building _____ the **light** and keeps the interior shaded and cool.

5. My professor asked me to _____ more statistical information **into** my paper.

6. The reason for her decision was **immediately** _____. We could see that she was exhausted.

7. The windows are small, but they provide **adequate** _____.

8. The company **regularly** _____ its Web site with news and information.

Multiword Vocabulary

A Find the words in bold in Reading 2. Then write the words that come before and/or after them to complete the multiword vocabulary.

1. _____ **way** _____ (Par. 1)

2. at the _____ _____ _____ **21st century** (Par. 2)

3. _____ _____ **same time** (Par. 4)

4. a breath of _____ _____ (Par. 6)

5. _____ this idea **in mind** (Par. 6)

6. extended _____ (Par. 7)

7. _____ **in touch** _____ (Par. 8)

8. _____ **keeping** _____ (Par. 8)

B Complete the following sentences with the correct multiword vocabulary from Exercise A. Use the information in parentheses to help you. In some cases, you need to change the verb form.

1. _____ (as one century was changing to the next), the United States was losing manufacturing plants to overseas locations.

2. When she went to Italy, she wanted to _____ (connect with) her family history, so she visited the town where her great grandparents were born.

3. It may take some time for soldiers to adjust when they return home. It is important for military families to _____ (remember).

4. The new library building is _____ (consistent with) the architecture of the rest of the buildings at the university.

5. After many years of similar television programs, this season brings _____ (change, new ideas).

6. It is important to stress hard work and high academic standards. _____ (what was just stated is true, and what follows is also true), schools should provide extra support for students who are not well prepared.

Dubai, United Arab Emirates

7. About one hundred trees in the park were cut down to _____ (clear a space for) a new building at the national university.

8. There are more than 50 people in her _____ (relatives including and beyond parents and children), including uncles, aunts, and cousins.

Use the Vocabulary

Write answers to the following questions. Use the words in bold in your answers. Then share your answers with a partner.

1. What do you think is the best way for young people to **get in touch with** their cultural traditions? Give examples.

2. Which traditional **elements** do you think people should **incorporate into** modern life?

3. In some cultures, the differences between the immediate and **extended family** are very **apparent**. Do they play different roles in your culture?

4. Where do you **draw inspiration from** when you want to do something creative—such as write or paint?

5. What aspects of daily life do you think will be different by the **turn of the** next **century**?

THINK AND DISCUSS

Work in a small group. Use the information in the reading and your own ideas to discuss the following questions.

1. **Relate to your knowledge.** Think of a new building in your community. Which elements are modern? Which elements are traditional? What do you like about the building and why?

2. **Evaluate.** Some architects believe that our perceptions of comfort have changed, for example, the inside temperatures we prefer. Do you think this is true? Explain your answer.

3. **Express an opinion.** Wang Shu believes that buildings have their own spirits. He sees them almost as living beings. What is your view?

Vocabulary Review

A Complete the reading with the vocabulary below that you have studied in the unit.

adequate ventilation	get in touch with	occupants of the building
at the same time	in keeping with	paid off
a breath of fresh air	innovative idea	withstand extreme temperatures
elaborate system		

In Zimbabwe, architects of a new office and shopping complex have brought

_____ to modern architecture. They

1

wanted to create an exciting, modern building.

_____, however, they wanted a

2

design that was _____ nature and

3

the building's location in southern Africa.

So, for inspiration, they turned to termites. Termites are insects that live in large colonies and eat wood, among other things. Termites live in gigantic earthen mounds that must be kept at a constant temperature. The termites are able to achieve this by using a(n)

_____ of heating and cooling vents.

4

The termites open and close the vents to regulate the temperature. Although the office complex in Zimbabwe is made of concrete, it operates on a similar principle, with a system of vents that bring in the outside air. The

Part of the building complex in Harare, Zimbabwe

office building has no air conditioning or heating, yet it provides _____. It

5

can _____ and still keep the many _____ comfortable all

6 7

year round.

This new and _____ has _____ in terms of energy

8 9

costs, which are 10 percent lower than traditional buildings of the same size. The building's

designers encourage others in their profession to _____ nature. They believe

10

we have a great deal to learn from nature's architects.

B Compare answers to Exercise A with a partner. Then discuss the following question.

What design principles did the architects take from termites?

C Complete the following sentences in a way that shows that you understand the meaning of the words in bold.

1. In my city, _____ is just a **fact of life**.

2. There was **discouraging news** about _____ on the radio today.

3. When I begin a new project, I always keep _____ **in mind**.

4. _____ is **beyond the means** of ordinary people.

D Work with a partner and write sentences that include any six of the vocabulary items below. You may use any verb tense and make nouns plural if you wish.

be prone to	immediately apparent	safeguard against
blend together	key element	say nothing of
don't stand a chance of	a matter of life and death	turn of the century
draw inspiration from		

Connect the Readings

A Look back at Readings 1 and 2 to complete the chart below. Put a check (✓) in the columns to show which topics appeared in each reading. Note that some topics overlap.

	Reading 1	Reading 2
1. The effect of materials on construction		
2. Construction that keeps occupants safe		
3. Respecting cultural tradition		
4. Using locally available or affordable materials		
5. Construction that keeps occupants comfortable		
6. Contrast between modern, high-tech construction and low-tech solutions		
7. Building projects in Asia		
8. Innovations in architecture and construction		

B With a partner or in a small group, compare your answers to Exercise A. Then discuss the following questions.

1. If a topic appeared in both readings, in which reading do you think the topic was more important? Why?

2. Both readings stress the importance of connecting to local communities and traditions. Do you think this means these communities are rejecting modern ways?

C Discuss the following questions with a partner. Use your understanding of the readings and your own ideas.

1. Is your community prone to earthquakes or other natural disasters? If so, do you think the buildings in your community will be able to withstand these disasters?

2. Describe the architecture in your city or community. Is its style traditional, modern, or a mix of both?

3. What kind of building do you live in?

4. What kind of architecture do you like? Would you prefer to live in a modern, high-rise building or a more traditional home? Explain your answer.

SEVEN

Genetics
and the

Human chromosomes that contain genetic material, magnified tens of thousands of times under a powerful electron microscope

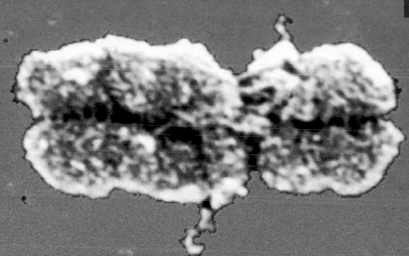
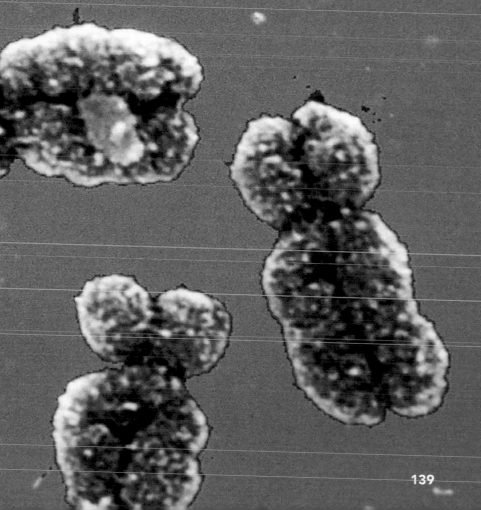

1. Do you have brothers, sisters, or cousins? How similar are they to you? To one another?

2. Do most children look like their parents? Do they act like them? Give reasons for your answers.

3. Do you think genes or the environment are responsible for these similarities? Explain your answer.

Environment

Academic Vocabulary

consistent	a label	a talent
to exaggerate	a phase	temporary
to inherit	subsequent	

Multiword Vocabulary

at random	in this respect
to draw distinctions	on one's own
to fall apart	an only child
to get into trouble	peer group

Some siblings have similar personalities, but many do not. Explore factors that influence sibling personalities and theories that explain them.

Reading Preview

A **Preview.** Read the first paragraph and the subheadings in Reading 1 on pages 142–143. With a partner, check (✓) four topics below that you think might be in this reading.

_____ **1.** Siblings with similar personalities

_____ **2.** Factors that shape our personalities

_____ **3.** Siblings who fight with each other

_____ **4.** The influence of the home environment on personality

_____ **5.** How expectations shape who we become

_____ **6.** Siblings with different personalities

B **Topic vocabulary.** The following words appear in Reading 1. Look at the words and answer the questions with a partner.

attention	expectations	praise
childhood	factors	research
circumstances	marriage	siblings
competition	personality	theory

1. Which words are most closely related to families?

2. Which words may relate to influences on a child's development?

3. What words suggest the reading will be scientific?

C **Predict.** What do you think this reading will be about? Discuss each word in Exercise B and predict how it may relate to the reading.

A boy carries his younger sister in Mongar, Bhutan.

Sibling Personalities

SIBLING
PERSONALITIES

Science tells us that we are 1
shaped by two fundamental
forces: our genes, which we
inherit from our parents, and our
environment, or the circumstances
in which we are raised. Based
on this explanation, you would
expect siblings to be quite similar.
Consider two brothers—let's call
them Paul and James—who are
now adults. They have the same
parents and they grew up in the
same home. Yet, as adults, the two
brothers could not be more different, according to their parents and
to the men themselves. How can
this happen?

Sylvester Stallone and
his brother, Frank

Paul was born first. As a child, he preferred 2
to spend time on his own or with a good friend,
but he was not comfortable in larger groups. He
was academically gifted,[1] responsible, and quiet.
His brother James was the youngest of four children. Unlike Paul, he did not care as much about
school. He was very popular and a leader in his
peer group, which was far more important to him
than school while he was growing up. In school,
he often got into trouble. Today, James sells adver-
tising for a large media company
and is politically conservative. He
plays golf and does volunteer work
at his church. Paul is a well-known
research scientist at a university.
He is politically liberal and his
hobbies include crossword puzzles
and long-distance running. All of
these things clearly demonstrate
the contrast in their personalities.

In this respect, these brothers are not 3
unusual, according to scientists who study
families. In terms of personality, siblings are
generally no more similar than two people
selected at random from the population. In
fact, recent studies indicate that siblings may

"In fact, recent studies indicate that siblings may actually be more different than a random pair of unrelated people."

actually be more different than a random pair of
unrelated people. Researchers suggest that this is
because the family environment may encourage
differences between siblings. The question is how
this happens. There are at least three competing
theories that attempt to answer this question.

Sibling Competition

The first theory suggests differences are the 4
result of children's competition for the love and
attention of their parents. It is easier to compete
successfully for your parents'
attention if you stand out in some
way. For example, a child who
does well in school or in sports
is likely to get praise and support
from his or her parents. However,
a child who behaves badly and
gets into trouble will also get a lot
of attention. So, if the first child
has established one way to get the
parents' attention, subsequent children may find
other ways. Because Paul was such a well-behaved
and successful student, James had to compete for
his parents' attention in a different way.

Home Environment

We assume that children from the same 5
family grow up in the same home environment.

---

[1] *gifted:* having a special talent to do something very well

However, a second theory of sibling differences indicates that this may not always be true. For example, in the case of the two brothers, when Paul was born, he was an only child and got lots of attention from his parents. By the time James was born eight years later, the house was full of noisy children. His parents' marriage was starting to fall apart. They divorced when James was four. His mother began working full-time and did not have much time for him. James rarely saw his father. All of these factors point to childhood environments that were very different for the two boys.

The Impact of Parents' Expectations

A final theory about sibling differences sug- 6 gests that, in early childhood, siblings are not really so different. Yet, parents often draw distinctions among their children; they sometimes exaggerate even relatively minor differences. So, perhaps, when James was small, he did not do very well in school and preferred to play with his friends. This might have been just a temporary phase in his life, but his parents decided he had social rather than academic talents. This label stuck and he began to act in ways that were consistent with this label and with his parents' expectations.

Scholars do not agree on which theory pro- 7 vides the best explanation for sibling differences. It is possible that they result from a combination of these factors. Experts do agree, however, there is more involved in sibling personalities than just genes and the environment.

READING COMPREHENSION

Big Picture

A Write the correct paragraph number(s) next to each of the following purposes. Note that item 2 relates to three paragraphs.

1. To give a detailed example that illustrates the scientific puzzle _____
2. To present a possible solution to the puzzle _____, _____, _____
3. To present a scientific puzzle that needs a solution _____
4. To generalize the puzzle beyond the illustrative example _____

B Read the following statements. Check (✓) the statement that expresses the main idea of the *whole* reading.

_____ 1. A home environment is very complex and is not always the same for each child.

_____ 2. Genes and environment alone cannot explain the differences between siblings.

_____ 3. Scholars don't really understand why siblings are often different.

Close-Up

A Choose the best answer for each of the following questions.

1. According to paragraph 1, which of the factors below has been shown to be the most important in determining who we become?
   a. Our experiences in school
   b. Our relationships with siblings
   c. Our genes

2. According to paragraph 3, which statement about siblings' personalities is true?
   a. They are usually very similar.
   b. They are often very different.
   c. They cannot be predicted at all.

3. Which statement is consistent with the *sibling competition* theory?
   a. Parents try to treat all their children in the same way.
   b. Children behave in certain ways to get their parents' attention and love.
   c. Children behave the way their parents expect them to behave.

4. How does the story of Paul and James illustrate the *home environment* theory?
   a. Other siblings have a strong influence on personality development.
   b. James's personality changed as he grew up.
   c. Paul and James experienced different home environments.

5. What can you infer about James from the *parents' expectations* theory?
   a. He became a sociable person because his parents encouraged this behavior.
   b. He didn't like the fact that his parents expected him to be sociable.
   c. He felt inferior to his brother.

Reading Skill

Analyzing Sentence Purpose

You have already learned that paragraphs have different purposes within a text. The same is often true of sentences. In good writing, individual sentences have a purpose: to introduce a problem, to offer an illustrative example, to make the reader question the assumption, and so on. Understanding the purpose of individual sentences can help you to comprehend the whole text better.

[1]Many American teenagers dream of leaving home and getting their own apartment in New York. [2]But a one-bedroom apartment in New York City costs more than $3000 a month. [3]So, more and more young adults are choosing to rent an apartment with someone from home—a sister or brother. [4]Because siblings grow up under the same roof, they are used to each other's habits. [5]So, they don't mind living in a smaller—and cheaper—apartment with a sibling.

In this paragraph:

Sentence 1 sets the reader's expectation about the topic—*young people want to leave home and get an apartment of their own.*

Sentence 2 poses a problem—*high cost.*

Sentence 3 offers a solution—*sharing rent with a sibling*, but also offers a contradiction since the first sentence said *they wanted to leave home.*

Sentences 4 and 5 explain why the solution works and resolves the contradiction.

Michael Jackson (middle) with his four brothers in California in 1977

A Read the sentences from paragraph 1 in Reading 1, which appear below. Match each sentence to its purpose. The first one has been done for you.

_b_ **1.** Science tells us that we are shaped by two fundamental forces: our genes, which we inherit from our parents, and our environment, or the circumstances in which we are raised.

_____ **2.** Based on this explanation, you would expect siblings to be quite similar.

_____ **3.** They have the same parents and they grew up in the same home.

_____ **4.** Yet, as adults, the two brothers could not be more different, according to their parents and to the men themselves.

_____ **5.** How can this happen?

a. This sentence offers an example that should fit the inference.

b. This sentence states a basic scientific assumption that many people share.

c. This sentence provides an inference based on this shared assumption.

d. This sentence asks a question that will be answered in the rest of the reading.

e. This sentence shows that the example contradicts the inference.

B Reread the beginning of paragraph 3 in Reading 1. Match each of the following sentences to its purpose. The first one has been done for you as an example.

_c_ **1.** In this respect, these brothers are not unusual, according to scientists who study families.

_____ **2.** In terms of personality, siblings are generally no more similar than two people selected at random from the population.

_____ **3.** In fact, recent studies indicate that siblings may actually be more different than a random pair of unrelated people.

_____ **4.** Researchers suggest that this is because the family environment may encourage differences between siblings.

a. This sentence answers the question at the end of paragraph 1.

b. The sentence extends the generalization even further with unexpected information.

c. This sentence connects this paragraph to the example in the previous paragraph.

d. The sentence generalizes the ideas beyond Paul and James's family to the rest of the population.

VOCABULARY PRACTICE

Academic Vocabulary

A Find the words in bold in Reading 1. Use the context and the sentences below to help you match each word to its correct definition.

_____ 1. We **inherit** (Par. 1) physical and personality traits from both parents.

_____ 2. We only have information for 2000–2005. We don't know anything about the **subsequent** (Par. 4) years.

_____ 3. This is a **temporary** (Par. 6) job. It is only for three months.

_____ 4. We are only in the first **phase** (Par. 6) of this project. We still have a lot of work to do.

_____ 5. People are born with different **talents** (Par. 6); for example, some are good at math, others are good at music.

_____ 6. Some experts don't like the **label** (Par. 6) "gifted." They say it makes children feel uncomfortable.

_____ 7. The design of the new building is **consistent** (Par. 6) with all the other buildings on the street. It has a similar style.

a. natural abilities

b. matching something else

c. continuing only for a limited time

d. word or phrase that describes someone or something

e. receive characteristics from parents through genes

f. step or stage in a process

g. happening after something else

B The academic words in bold often appear with the words in the box. Complete the sentences below. One word is not used.

as	from	in	next	only	with

1. The _____ **phase** in the road construction project will begin in January.

2. The laws of government are not always **consistent** _____ religious ideas.

3. We **inherit** many traits _____ our parents.

4. He attended a special school for students with **talent** _____ math and science.

5. This address is _____ **temporary**. I plan to move in a few weeks.

Multiword Vocabulary

A Find the multiword vocabulary in bold in Reading 1 and use the context to help you figure out the meaning. Then match each item to the correct definition.

_____ 1. **on his own** (Par. 2)

_____ 2. **peer group** (Par. 2)

_____ 3. **got into trouble** (Par. 2)

_____ 4. **in this respect** (Par. 3)

_____ 5. **at random** (Par. 3)

_____ 6. **an only child** (Par. 5)

_____ 7. **fall apart** (Par. 5)

_____ 8. **draw distinctions** (Par. 6)

a. a group of people of about the same age and class

b. someone who has no siblings

c. without other people

d. got into a situation where people were angry at you

e. say that two things are different

f. without a plan or pattern

g. have so many problems that something no longer works

h. relating to something that has just been mentioned

B Complete the following sentences using the correct multiword vocabulary from Exercise A. In some cases, you need to change the word form.

1. She grew up as _____ and always wished she had a little brother or sister.

2. It is important to _____ between what you want and what you need.

3. The name of the winner was chosen _____ by a computer.

4. People who don't like to follow the rules often _____ .

5. Food and safety are our most basic needs. _____ , human beings are not very different from other animals.

6. Although many assignments require students to work in groups, some students prefer to work _____ .

7. Teenagers often pay little attention to their parents. For them, their _____ is often the most important influence in their lives.

8. The business started to _____ soon after the original owner died. By the next year, it closed down.

Use the Vocabulary

Write answers to the following questions. Use the words in bold in your answers. Then share your answers with a partner.

1. Describe a time when you **got into trouble** when you were a child.

2. Do you think your parents gave you a **label** when you were a child? If so, what was it?

3. Do you have a **talent** in a particular area?

4. How important was your **peer group** when you were growing up? Do you think the importance of the peer group was just a **temporary phase**? How important is your peer group now?

5. Do you like to do schoolwork with classmates or do you prefer to work **on your own**?

6. What is the most obvious trait you have **inherited from** your mother? Your father?

THINK AND DISCUSS

Work in a small group. Use the information in the reading and your own ideas to discuss the following questions.

1. **Evaluate.** Which theory of sibling difference do you think makes the most sense? Why?

2. **Apply knowledge.** Do any of the theories help explain differences between you and your siblings or between siblings in another family that you know well?

3. **Give an opinion.** How much do you think that labels affect children? Adults?

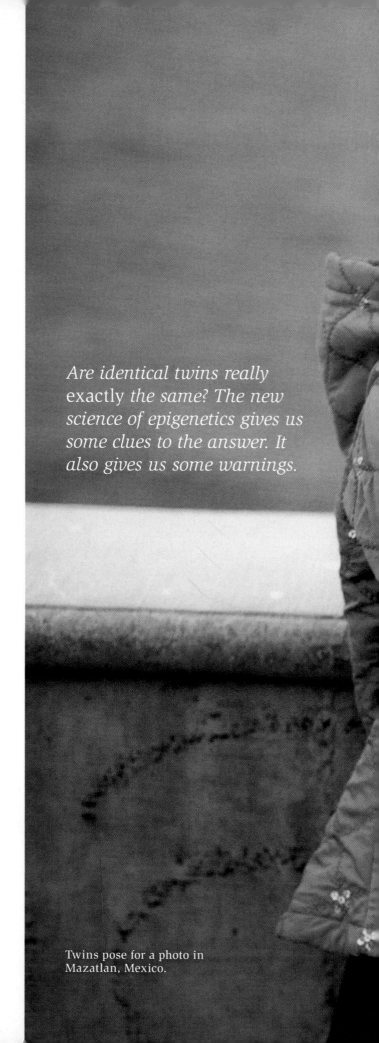

Academic Vocabulary

to alter	obesity	to suppress
complementary	radical	to untangle
isolated	stress	

Multiword Vocabulary

after all	to have an impact on
anything but	in this case
to be forced to conclude	on the cutting edge
to come into play	to pass something on to

Reading Preview

A **Preview.** Read the first sentence of each paragraph in Reading 2. Then discuss the following questions with a partner or in a small group.

1. Why do you think scientists are interested in twins?

2. What two terms do you think will be explained in the reading?

3. What do we pass on to our children through our genes?

B **Topic vocabulary.** The following words appear in Reading 2. Look at the words and answer the questions with a partner.

biochemical	diet	grandchildren
cancer	DNA	toxins
cell	generation	twins
development	genetic	

1. Which words are connected to families?

2. Which words are related to health?

3. What words are scientific terms?

C **Predict.** What do you think this reading will be about? Discuss each word in Exercise B and predict how it may relate to the reading.

Are identical twins really exactly *the same?* The new science of epigenetics gives us some clues to the answer. It also gives us some warnings.

Twins pose for a photo in Mazatlan, Mexico.

Epigenetics

E very summer, on the first weekend in 1
August, thousands of twins converge on
Twinsburg, Ohio, a small town named
by identical twin brothers nearly two centuries
ago. They come, two by two, for the Twins
Days Festival, the world's largest gathering
of twins.

Twins are not the only people who are regu- 2
lar festival visitors. There are also several groups
of scientists. To these scientists, identical twins

offer a precious opportunity to untangle the influence of genes and the environment. Although
identical twins look exactly alike to most people,
they differ in many small ways, and these differences increase with age. For example, one may
develop wrinkles on her face, but the other does
not. They may also differ in more dramatic ways.
One may die of cancer at age 50 and the other
may live a healthy life until 85. Because identical
twins share virtually the same genes, it has been

Twins gather at the Twins Days Festival in Twinsburg, Ohio, USA.

of genes, which is composed of DNA. The epigenome ("above the genes") controls genes. It is a complex set of biochemical controls, called tags, that does not alter genes but can turn genes on or off. Epigenetics is the study of epigenomes and how they shape who we are. (See Figure 1 on page 152.)

To understand epigenetics, think of our DNA 4
as a script[1] for a play. Every actor—in this case, every gene—has the same script. However, each actor has a different role to play and different words to say. Like a play script, epigenetic tags can determine the role that each cell plays. For example, even though every cell contains the same DNA, one may become a muscle cell and another may become a skin cell. These epigenetic tags can also control which genes are turned on, or expressed, and which are turned off, or suppressed. This is a normal part of development. Some epigenetic changes, however, are anything but normal. For example, an epigenetic change may turn off a gene for proper cell growth, leading to cancer or obesity.

Scientists are not entirely sure why these 5
harmful epigenetic changes occur, but they are sure that the environment plays a big part. The environment includes your physical surroundings as well as what you eat, drink, and do. Scientists believe that your behavioral choices can lead to epigenetic changes. These choices include your diet, whether you smoke, or even how much time you spend in the sun. Epigenetic changes may also be caused by factors you cannot always control, such as toxins in your environment or high stress. These changes explain why identical twins grow more different as they age. Their environments, behaviors, and life experiences are not exactly the same.

None of this was terribly surprising to scien- 6
tists at the Twins Days Festival, who have long known that the environment and behavioral choices have an impact on health. What has astonished scientists is that these effects could be passed on to the next generation. This was surprising because genes and the environment had

thought that differences between twins are due to environmental factors.

Lately, however, studies of identical twins 3
have led scientists who are working on the cutting edge of genetics research to a different and radical new conclusion: Genes and the environment are not the only fundamental forces at work. According to recent research, a third factor also comes into play: the epigenome. (The prefix *epi-* means "above.") A genome is a complete set

---

[1] *script:* all of the words that actors say in a play, written down in the form of a book

always been considered complementary but independent factors. However, with the discovery of the epigenome they were forced to conclude that these two factors are not completely independent after all. For example, if epigenetic changes lead to obesity in parents, they may pass this change on to their children. This was seen in a study of several generations of residents in an isolated part of Sweden. This surprised scientists because they had always believed that the choices made by one generation would not affect the next generation.

It turns out this is not the case. Although the environment cannot alter the genetic code, it can change gene expression—the position of the on-off switch—in future generations. This means that it is not just the choices that a mother makes during pregnancy that are significant for the child's future health. The choices that both the mother and father make are important, and long before they start a family. As a famous quote states, "You are what you eat." It seems that you may also be what your mother, father, and even grandparents ate . . . and drank, and smoked.

AN EARLY STUDY IN EPIGENETICS

A story that is on the cutting edge of modern science began in an isolated part of northern Sweden in the 19th century. This area of the country had unpredictable harvests through the first half of the century. In years that the harvest failed, the population went hungry. However, the good years were very good. The same people who went hungry during bad harvests overate significantly during the good years. A Swedish scientist wondered about the long-term effects of these eating patterns. He studied the harvest and health records of the area. He was astonished by what he found. Boys who overate during the good years produced children and grandchildren who died about six years earlier than the children and grandchildren of those who had very little to eat. Other scientists found the same result for girls. The scientists were forced to conclude that just one season of overeating could have a negative impact that continued for generations. In other words, environmental conditions altered gene expression, establishing new traits within a generation.

Figure 1. Same Genes, Different People

Identical twins are born with the same DNA but can become surprisingly different as they mature. A growing field called epigenetics is revealing how factors like stress and nutrition can cause this difference by changing how individual genes behave.

Gene expression over time ▶

Twin 1

Twin 2

Identical DNA is not altered by tags.

Varying tags make twins different.

Epigenetic tag
Tags are chemical mechanisms that change gene expression; that is, they can turn genes on and off. They do not change DNA. Scientists expect that changed tags can be inherited.

What causes tags to change?
Environmental influence such as nutrition may change tags. This can change gene expression.

READING COMPREHENSION

Big Picture

A Choose the best answer for each of the following questions.

1. Which sentence expresses the main idea of paragraph 2?
   a. The first sentence   **b.** The third sentence   **c.** The last sentence

2. What is the main idea of paragraph 3?
   a. Epigenetics may explain what genes and environment alone cannot explain.
   b. The epigenome is more important than either genes or the environment.
   c. Epigenetics is a study of identical twins and the environment.

3. What is the purpose of paragraph 4?
   a. To give a definition of the epigenome
   b. To prove that epigenetic processes cause cancer
   c. To explain how epigenetic processes control genes

4. What is the main idea of paragraph 5?
   a. Identical twins do not really have identical genes.
   b. Smoking and stress can alter your genes.
   c. The environment and behavior can lead to epigenetic changes.

5. What is the main idea of paragraph 6?
   a. The impact of people's choices may extend beyond their own lives to future generations.
   b. Fathers need to be careful about diet because their choices affect their health.
   c. Epigenetics can affect your environment and the environment of your children.

B Number these events to show the correct order, according to the reading.

_____ **1.** Gene expression changes.

_____ **2.** Person experiences environmental factors (such as stress) and makes behavioral choices (such as smoking).

_____ **3.** Changes occur in a person's health (such as obesity or cancer).

_____ **4.** Epigenetic changes occur; that is, changes occur in tags on genes.

Close-Up

A Decide which of the following statements are true or false according to Reading 2 and the short extra reading, "An Early Study in Epigenetics," on page 152. Write *T* (True) or *F* (False) next to each one.

_____ **1.** Identical twins are completely identical.

_____ **2.** Epigenetic tags control gene expression.

_____ **3.** Epigenetic changes can lead to disease.

_____ **4.** The environment can alter your genes.

_____ **5.** Epigenetic changes can be inherited.

_____ **6.** The Swedish study showed that epigenetic changes are limited to the next generation.

B Work with a partner or in a small group. Change the false statements in Exercise A to make them true.

Reading Skill

A Review the supplementary material "An Early Study in Epigenetics" on page 152. What do you think the general purpose of this material is? _____

B Read the following statements from the main text. Check (✓) the ones that are discussed and supported in the supplementary material in the box on page 152.

_____ **1.** Twins share virtually the same genes. (Par. 2)

_____ **2.** Even though every cell contains the same DNA, one may become a muscle cell and another may become a skin cell. (Par. 4)

_____ **3.** Scientists believe that your behavioral choices can lead to epigenetic changes. (Par. 5)

_____ **4.** What has astonished scientists is that these effects could be passed on to the next generation. (Par. 6)

_____ **5.** The choices that a mother makes during pregnancy are significant for the child's future health. (Par. 7)

VOCABULARY PRACTICE

Academic Vocabulary

A Find the words in bold in Reading 1. Use the context and the sentences below to help you match each word to its definition.

_____ **1.** Engineers hope that the new roads will **untangle** (Par. 2) the terrible traffic in the city.

_____ **2.** The statement that "all men are created equal" was a **radical** (Par. 3) idea in the 18th century. It was not generally accepted until much later.

_____ **3.** Many scientists believe that human activity can **alter** (Par. 3) our climate. In particular, they believe it is getting warmer.

_____ **4.** He **suppressed** (Par. 4) his anger until the end of the meeting, but then he lost his temper and began to shout.

_____ **5.** **Obesity** (Par. 4) is a huge problem in the United States. More than 35 percent of adults are extremely overweight.

_____ **6.** Many parents complain that the responsibilities of work and family create a lot of **stress** (Par. 5) in their lives.

_____ **7.** The company hired two new employees with **complementary** (Par. 6) skills. One was good at writing and the other knew a lot about technology.

_____ **8.** It is difficult for workers to reach the new factory because it is far from the city in a very **isolated** (Par. 6) area.

a. useful or beneficial together

b. far away and separate from other things

c. stopped something from happening or developing

d. extremely different and new

e. the state of being extremely fat

f. change

g. continuous feelings of worry about work or personal problems

h. separate out things or ideas so they become less complicated

B Choose an academic word from the box to complete each of the following sentences. Notice and learn the words in bold because they often appear with the academic words.

alter	isolated	radical	suppress
complementary	obesity	stress	untangle

1. We have to finish the project by next week, so everyone is in the office is **under** a lot of _____.

2. Unfortunately, the _____ **rate** is rising every year. The number of children who are overweight is of special concern.

3. Genetics and the environment have _____ **roles** in determining our health.

4. After our parents died, we had to _____ the financial **mess** that they had left. Their bank and insurance records were disorganized and incomplete.

5. The accident took place in a(n) _____ **area**, so it took a long time for the police to arrive.

6. The new president has made some _____ **changes** in the company. Things are going to be very different from now on.

7. She couldn't _____ her **smile** when she read the good news.

8. These ideas will **fundamentally** _____ how we teach math and science.

Multiword Vocabulary

A Find the words in bold in Reading 2. Then write the words that come before and/or after them to complete the multiword vocabulary.

1. on _____ _____ **edge** (Par. 3)

2. _____ **into play** (Par. 3)

3. _____ _____ **case** (Par. 4)

4. _____ **but** (Par. 4)

5. have an _____ _____ (Par. 6)

6. _____ **on to** (Par. 6)

7. were **forced** _____ _____ (Par. 6)

8. _____ **all** (Par. 6)

B Complete the following sentences with the correct multiword vocabulary from Exercise A. Use the information in parentheses to help you. In some cases, you need to change the verb form.

1. The scientists at the university work _____ (involved in the most exciting new developments) of genetic research.

2. Some behavior, such as smoking and overeating, may _____ (have an effect on) future generations.

3. I looked everywhere for my earring—at home, in the car, at my office—but could not find it. I _____ (decide that something is true based on evidence that you don't really want to accept) that I had lost it.

4. Everyone thought it was going to rain today, but it turned out to be a nice day _____ (in spite of what was expected).

5. Many factors _____ (have an effect or become important) when voters have to decide which candidate they prefer.

6. The teacher promised the instructions for the assignment would be clear and easy to follow, but I found that they were _____ (not in any way) clear.

7. Hair color is one trait that parents can _____ (give) their children.

8. On January 1, we will have to follow a new law. I am usually in favor of laws that support small businesses, but _____ (in this situation), I am not.

Use the Vocabulary

Write answers to the following questions. Use the words in bold in your answers. Then share your answers with a partner.

1. What basic ideas and values do you want to **pass on to** your children? What factors do you think **come into play** when children and teenagers make important decisions? Do these factors change when they are **under stress**?

2. Do you think parents or peer groups **have the** greatest **impact on** how children and teenagers behave? Do you think their influence is **complementary**? Or, do they work against each other? Explain your answer.

3. Some developing countries are beginning to have the same high **obesity rates** as developed countries. Is there anything that can be done to **alter** this trend?

4. Many children around the world go hungry every day. The United Nations Children's Fund (UNICEF) works to prevent hunger among the world's children. With your partner, offer some **radical** ideas that might help in their work.

THINK AND DISCUSS

Work in a small group. Use the information in the reading and your own ideas to discuss the following questions.

1. **Summarize.** What are the primary new findings from epigenetic research?

2. **Apply knowledge.** Epigenetic research has shown that behavioral choices and environmental factors can have an important impact on health. How do you think this new information should affect government programs and policies? Make one recommendation that a responsible government should follow, based on your new knowledge.

3. **Relate to personal experience.** How might this new information affect choices in your own life? Do you think it will change your behavior? Explain your answer.

Vocabulary Review

A Complete the reading with the vocabulary below that you have studied in the unit.

after all	inherit from
comes into play	next phase
complementary roles	pass on
consistent with	radical changes
fundamentally alter	were forced to conclude

Iraqi boys taking a test in Baghdad, Iraq, 2007

Throughout much of the 20th century, scientists and education experts tried to determine the contributions of genes and the environment to intelligence. The answer is important for decisions about education. For example, if the environment can _____ 1 intelligence, the government should make an effort to improve the environment in which children learn. However, if intelligence is something we _____ 2 our parents, then it may not be worthwhile to try to improve the learning environment. After years of research, scientists _____ 3 that about 75 percent of intelligence is genetic.

However, during the _____ 4 of intelligence research came a surprise. New results were not _____ 5 the earlier studies. The new studies showed that the two factors are not in opposition _____ 6. Instead, scientists began to see them as playing _____ 7 in explaining intelligence. They now believe that parents do _____ 8 genes for intelligence to their children. However, the genetic portion of intelligence is only potential intelligence. Experts currently believe that genes define the limits of intelligence, but then the environment _____ 9. The environment determines if a person will be able to reach those limits. This insight could lead to _____ 10 in how we approach education.

B Compare answers to Exercise A with a partner. Then discuss the following question.

How do you think this new research could change our approach to education?

C Complete the following sentences in a way that shows that you understand the meaning of the words in bold.

1. It's hard to be an **only child** because _____.

2. When I speak in English, I sometimes **get into trouble** when _____.

3. He chose to live **on his own** because _____.

4. If you are **under** a lot of **stress** at work, you should _____.

D Work with a partner and write sentences that include any six of the vocabulary items below. You may use any verb tense and make nouns plural if you wish.

anything but	fall apart	isolated area	on the cutting edge
at random	have an impact on	only temporary	peer group
draw distinctions	in this respect		

Connect the Readings

A Work with a partner. Consider what you have learned about identical twins and siblings who are not twins. What factors contribute to similarities and differences between twins and among siblings? Fill out the chart below with checks (✓) in the appropriate columns.

	Identical Twins		Non-Twin Siblings	
	Similarities	Differences	Similarities	Differences
Genes contribute to . . .				
The environment contributes to . . .				
Epigenetic processes contribute to . . .				

B With a partner or in a small group, compare answers to Exercise A. Then follow the steps below.

1. Make a list of four or five factors in the environment that may contribute to similarities and differences in Exercise A. For example, one factor is diet.

   _____   _____

   _____   _____

   _____

2. For each factor, write a sentence explaining how it contributes to similarities or differences. For example:

   Diet is an important environmental factor. For example, a twin who has an unhealthy diet may die

   long before his or her twin who has a healthy diet.

   _____

   _____

   _____

   _____

C Discuss the following questions with a partner. Use your understanding of the readings and your own ideas.

1. How has what you have read in this unit changed your understanding of your family members? Could it have an influence on how you raise your own children? Explain your answer.

2. Has what you have read in this unit made you think any differently about your past behavior or decisions? Explain your answer.

A woman rides
a unicycle in
Shanghai, China.
The unicycle was
designed by Chinese
inventor Li Yongli.

INVENTIONS

1. Are there important inventions that originated in your country or community? What are they?

2. What do you consider to be the most important invention of the last 100 years? Why do you think so?

Academic Vocabulary

a component	hygiene	to tackle
a compound	massive	vibrant
to convert	to sustain	

Multiword Vocabulary

at an angle	from far and wide
at the heart of	it comes as no surprise
at the height of	that
one's power	to lay the foundation for
to draw on	to make one's mark

Explore this period of great accomplishment in science and engineering. Read about machines and everyday objects that have their origin in this golden age of discovery and invention.

Reading Preview

(A) Preview. Read the title and subheadings in Reading 1. Then discuss the following questions with a partner.

1. What do you think is the meaning of "Golden Age" in the title?

2. The subheadings have the form "from X to Y." Why do you think the author used this form?

3. Name some inventions that you think the reading will discuss.

(B) Topic vocabulary. The following words appear in Reading 1. Look at the words and answer the questions with a partner.

astronomy	discovery	optics
chemistry	gasoline	perfume
cosmetics	machines	shampoo
deodorant	method	techniques

1. Which words are connected to the invention process?

2. Which words are related to science and technology?

3. How are the words *cosmetics*, *deodorant*, *perfume*, and *shampoo* related? How might chemistry be involved in them?

(C) Predict. What do you think this reading will be about? Discuss each word in Exercise B and predict how it may relate to the reading.

An Islamic design for a water-powered clock from the 13th century

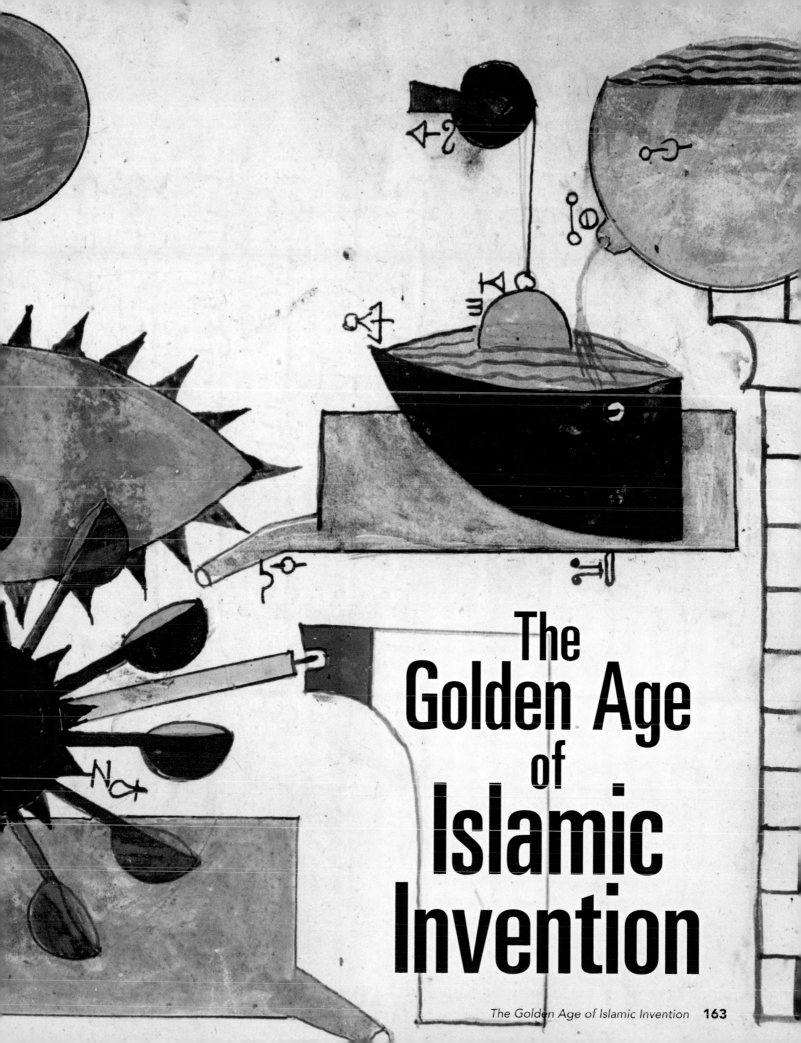

The Golden Age of Islamic Invention

THE GOLDEN AGE OF ISLAMIC INVENTION

[1] The Dark Ages, we are told, was a time of economic and cultural collapse in Europe. This period, between the end of the Classical Age[1] (900 BCE to 600 CE[2]) and the beginning of the Renaissance[3] (1300–1600 CE), may have been dark in most of Europe. However, to the east, across the Islamic world, this period was anything but dark. To the contrary, from the 7th century to the time of the European Renaissance, Islamic civilization experienced an explosion of culture and scientific thought and discovery. For more than six hundred years, it was the world's center of learning. Scientists, philosophers, artists, and engineers sustained and extended the knowledge of the classical world, and laid the foundation for the European Renaissance. Consider some essential objects of our daily lives, among them gasoline, plastic, cars, cameras, and soap. Many of them have their origins in inventions of this Golden Age of Islam.

[2] In the 12th century, the Islamic world was enormous. It stretched from Spain, across North Africa, all the way east to present-day Pakistan.

---

[1] *Classical Age:* a period of history in which Greece and Rome held enormous political power and cultural influence

[2] *CE:* abbreviation for *Common Era*. It indicates the number of years after year 1 of the calendar used in Europe and the Americas. (For BCE, see footnote on page 39.)

[3] *Renaissance:* a period in European history in which there were many artistic, cultural, and scientific developments

Within its borders were many languages, cultures, and traditions. At the height of its power, it also was home to a massive, vibrant economy, which fueled exploration and the growth of knowledge. Scholars from far and wide converged on Baghdad, Cairo, Tripoli, and Cordoba, which were centers of learning and scientific research and discovery. News of the ideas and inventions of the Islamic world found its way through Europe over trade routes. It also traveled back from the east with the soldiers returning from the Crusades.[4] The following are three of the hundreds of inventions that have made their mark on the world.

---

[4] *Crusades:* a series of wars from the 11th through 13th centuries led by Christians against Muslims

An ox-powered water wheel, seen here in Egypt, circa 1947

From Irrigation[5] to Engines

In many parts of the world, irrigation is at the heart of successful agriculture. Various methods of irrigation had been developed all over the world. However, no one had found a way to raise water from below ground without great effort. A brilliant engineer in Turkey at the beginning of the 13th century, Al-Jazari, decided to tackle the problem. He used existing technology to create the crank-connecting rod system. A crank is a long bar that is attached at a right angle to a rotating rod. One end of the rod moves in a circle. The other end slides up and down. This system was an important advance because it converts circular motion into linear motion. With this device, an ox walking in a circle could raise water to the surface. The same system is used today in a wide range of machines, including bicycles and car engines.

From Perfume to Gasoline

Some of the most significant scientific advances during this period were in chemistry. As early as the 9th century, chemists in Iraq and Iran were developing basic equipment and chemical techniques. Many are still in use today. One of the most important of these techniques was distillation. This is a method of separating out different components of a liquid mixture. It uses the differences in the boiling point of each component in the mixture. When each component boils, it changes into a gas. Each gas is then collected in a separate container. When the gases cool, they turn back into liquid, but in the separate containers. This technique was used to create perfumes, vinegar, and alcohol, which was used as a disinfectant.[6] Today, distillation is an essential step in the production of gasoline, plastic, and many medicines.

Hygiene: From the Mosque to the Home

For Muslims, hygiene is a religious matter. They must wash before they enter the mosque for prayers. It comes as no surprise that Arab chemists were busy finding the best way to wash.

---

[5] *irrigation:* a system of providing water so that plants will grow

[6] *disinfectant:* a chemical that destroys bacteria and that can prevent diseases from spreading

Why is this a job for a chemist? In the ancient world, people used oils to clean their bodies. However, because oil and water do not blend, this was not a very effective method. Oil can help remove the dirt, but water cannot rinse away the dirty oil. Arab chemists were the first to create a water-soluble[7] compound, which was very effective for cleaning. Today, we call that compound soap. Chemists also created shampoo as well as

cosmetics, mouthwash, and deodorant. In contrast, soap, and personal hygiene in general, did not become an accepted part of European culture until well into the 18th century.

There were hundreds of other discoveries and inventions that were influential in the fields of astronomy, engineering, mathematics, medicine, and optics, as well as architecture and music. It is thought that later, many western scholars, including Roger Bacon, Nicolaus Copernicus, Leonardo da Vinci, and Isaac Newton, all drew on the work of the scholars of the Golden Age of Islam.

6

---

[7] *water-soluble:* able to become liquid when mixed with water

READING COMPREHENSION

Big Picture

Ⓐ Read the following groups of sentences. In each group, one sentence is a main idea. The other sentences are supporting details. Write *MI* next to the main idea. Write *SD* next to the supporting details.

1. Paragraph 1
   _____ a. From the 7th to the 14th centuries, there were significant scientific developments in the Islamic world.
   _____ b. The European Renaissance drew ideas from the Islamic world.
   _____ c. We still rely on many ideas from the Islamic Golden Age.

2. Paragraph 2
   _____ a. Soldiers who fought in the Crusades brought ideas back to Western Europe from the Islamic world.
   _____ b. During the Golden Age, the Islamic empire was the world's center of learning and science.
   _____ c. The Islamic empire was massive.

3. Paragraph 3
   _____ a. Al-Jazari made a breakthrough in agriculture.
   _____ b. The basic design of the crank-connecting rod is still in use today.
   _____ c. Al-Jazari used technology to solve a problem that had existed for a long time.

4. Paragraph 4
   _____ a. Islamic chemists invented chemical equipment.
   _____ b. Distillation is used in the manufacture of plastics and fuels.
   _____ c. One of the most important advances in chemistry was distillation.

5. Paragraph 5
   _____ a. Europeans did not use personal hygiene products until much later.
   _____ b. The accomplishments of Islamic chemists included many products to improve personal hygiene.
   _____ c. Muslims must wash before entering a mosque.

B Read the following sentences. Which sentence is the main idea of the *whole* reading? Which sentences are supporting details? Write *MI* next to the main idea and *SD* next to the details.

_____ **a.** Many western scholars used ideas and inventions that were developed during the Golden Age of Islam.

_____ **b.** Some of the most significant accomplishments of the Golden Age were in chemistry.

_____ **c.** A significant number of important inventions, many of which are still relevant today, were developed during the Golden Age of Islam.

Close-Up

A Decide which of the following statements are true or false according to the reading. Write *T* (True) or *F* (False) next to each one.

_____ **1.** Islamic scholars based many of their inventions on ideas from the Renaissance.

_____ **2.** Scientific news traveled west from the Islamic world along trade routes.

_____ **3.** The crank-connecting rod system had an important impact on agriculture.

_____ **4.** Distillation was a new technique for the development of water-soluble compounds.

_____ **5.** Mouthwash was invented during the Golden Age of Islam.

_____ **6.** Islamic scholars studied the ideas of Leonardo da Vinci.

B Work with a partner or in a small group. Change the false statements in Exercise A to make them true.

Reading Skill

Scanning

Sometimes when you read, you are looking for the answer to a specific question. You may be studying for a test or writing a paper and you need to find this information. If you have a question in mind before you begin to read, you can scan the text for the answer and avoid getting lost in a text that contains a lot of new information. Scanning helps you focus as you read.

When you scan, you don't have to read the text carefully. Instead, you should move your eyes quickly down the page looking for the following clues that can answer your question.

Names: look for names of people and places, which begin with capital letters

Dates: look for years, months, and days of the week

Numbers: look for words that signify numbers, percentages, and statistics

Key Words: look for words in italics, bold, quotation marks, or words that are defined in the text

A Read each of the following questions and write down what kind of clue you will scan for. The first one has been done for you. Then scan the paragraph on the next page to find the answers and add them to the chart.

Questions	Clue	Answer
1. Who invented Post-it Notes?	*names*	
2. When was the glue for the notes first invented?		
3. What company sells them?		
4. Why were the first Post-it Notes yellow?		
5. In how many countries is the product sold?		

Did you ever wonder who invented Post-it Notes, those little pieces of paper that you can stick on things, take off, and then stick on something else? Believe it or not, their invention was an accident. In 1968, Spencer Silver, a chemist at 3M, a large company in the United States, was trying to create a new kind of glue. He was trying to make a very strong glue, but he failed. Instead, he ended up creating a kind of glue that could attach to paper several times without leaving any messy glue behind when you remove it. No one was very interested in his invention, but he kept promoting it among his colleagues at the company. In 1974, one of those colleagues, Arthur Fry, thought the glue was a solution to a problem he was having. His bookmarks always fell out of his books. He wanted a bookmark that would stick but would not damage the book. He thought that Silver's glue would fit the bill. He tried it and it worked perfectly. In a short time, everyone in the company was using Fry's "bookmarks" to mark their documents. Soon the 3M company decided to try to sell the new invention. They had a lot of yellow paper left from another project so they made the new product in yellow. In 1980, they began to sell these little yellow pads of sticky paper as Post-it Notes. Today, there are more than 1,000 different Post-it Note products sold in over 150 countries.

B Scan Reading 1 to find the answers to the following questions. Before you scan for the answer to each question, write down what kind of clue you are looking for.

Question	Clue	Answer
1. When was the Renaissance?		
2. What were some important cities in the Islamic world during the Golden Age?		
3. Who was Al-Jazari?		
4. What was one important advance in chemistry at that time?		
5. Why was soap different from early forms of personal hygiene?		
6. Which western scholars based some of their work on ideas from the Golden Age of Islam?		

VOCABULARY PRACTICE

Academic Vocabulary

A Find the words in the box below in Reading 1. Use the context to help you complete each of the following sentences. Use the information in parentheses to help you.

sustained (Par. 1)	vibrant (Par. 2)	converts (Par. 3)	hygiene (Par. 5)
massive (Par. 2)	tackle (Par. 3)	components (Par. 4)	compound (Par. 5)

1. Exercise and diet are important _____ (parts, pieces) of a healthy lifestyle.

2. The modern toothbrush was an important advance in dental _____ (practice of keeping clean).

3. Food from their garden _____ (kept them going) them during the war when there was little to eat.

4. Heat _____ (changes) water into steam.

5. We are expecting a _____ (very large) storm later today, so all of the airports in the region are closed.

6. We are looking for employees who are ready to _____ (deal with) new challenges.

7. Water is a _____ (combination of two or more substances) made up of oxygen and hydrogen molecules.

8. The newest models of television have _____ (brilliant) colors and realistic sound.

B Work with a partner and match the words in bold to words that they may combine with. Give reasons for your choices.

_____ 1. **convert**   **a.** amount

_____ 2. key   **b.** colors

_____ 3. **massive**   **c.** **hygiene**

_____ 4. chemical   **d.** into

_____ 5. **tackle**   **e.** the growth

_____ 6. personal   **f.** **component**

_____ 7. **vibrant**   **g.** the problem

_____ 8. **sustain**   **h.** **compound**

C Choose word combinations from Exercise B to complete each of the following sentences. In some cases, you need to change the verb or noun form.

1. You can _____ Euros _____ dollars at the airport.

2. Secrecy is a _____ _____ of this plan. It is very important that nobody find out about it.

3. The teacher assigned a _____ _____ of homework this week. None of the students was able to finish it.

4. The scientists invented a new _____ _____ that may be useful in the oil industry in the future.

5. It is time for us to _____ _____ and find an appropriate solution for it.

6. There has been a tremendous increase in the number of _____ _____ products including, soaps, shampoos, and makeup.

7. All the houses on the island were painted with _____ _____.

8. The new government policy is designed to _____ _____ of the economy.

Multiword Vocabulary

A Find the multiword vocabulary in bold in Reading 1. Use the context to help match each one to its definition.

_____ 1. **laid the foundation for** (Par. 1)   **a.** used

_____ 2. **at the height of its power** (Par. 2)   **b.** from many different places

_____ 3. **from far and wide** (Par. 2)   **c.** when something is strongest

_____ 4. **made** their **mark** (Par. 2)   **d.** had an impact

_____ 5. **at the heart of** (Par. 3)   **e.** at 90 degrees

_____ 6. **at a** right **angle** (Par. 3)   **f.** made the next step easier

_____ 7. **it comes as no surprise that** (Par. 5)   **g.** central to

_____ 8. **drew on** (Par. 6)   **h.** it is clear from what has already been said

B Complete the following sentences with the correct multiword vocabulary from Exercise A. In some cases, you need to change the word form.

1. Research in basic science often _____ advances in medicine.

2. Trust is _____ all successful relationships.

3. He never did his homework and rarely studied, so _____ he failed the final exam.

4. Young people sometimes leave their hometowns to _____ in the world.

5. The garage was built _____ to the house.

6. Authors often _____ their own experiences when they write fiction.

7. _____, Britain had one of the largest empires in history.

8. People came from _____ to hear the candidates' debate.

Use the Vocabulary

Write answers to the following questions. Use the words in bold in your answers. Then share your answers with a partner.

1. What do you do when you have to **tackle a difficult problem**? Do you **draw on** your inner strength? Rely on friends for advice? Do research on the problem? What **sustains** your motivation to continue?

2. Think of a **vibrant** city or community that you know well. What do you think is **at the heart of** its character?

3. Think ahead 25 years from now and imagine what your life will be. Where and how do you hope that you will have **made your mark**?

4. Groups that have not always been well represented in government or business (e.g., women or minority groups) often point to a particular person who **laid the foundation** for the careers of others like them. For example, Jackie Robinson was the first African American to play in Major League Baseball. He made it easier for African-American athletes who came later. Who are some other similar pioneers?

5. In your view, what are the **key components** of success?

THINK AND DISCUSS

Work in a small group. Use the information in the reading and your own ideas to discuss the following questions.

1. **Use prior knowledge.** What information in the reading surprised you? Explain your answer.

2. **Apply knowledge.** One of the inventions described in the reading was distillation. Why do you think this was so important? How and where is distillation used today?

3. **Express an opinion.** Some scholars maintain that the accomplishments of the Islamic world have been minimized and that we tend to focus on the accomplishments of the western world. Do you think this is the case? Explain your answer.

Academic Vocabulary

to diagnose	to exhibit	to quit
to elevate	a lens	a sphere
to enchant	a manual	

Multiword Vocabulary

to come to the realization that	a pad of paper
	a practical application
to do the trick	some sort of
to end up	these days
to have the potential	

Reading Preview

A **Preview.** Read the title of Reading 2. Look at the photos on pages 172–175 and read their captions. Then discuss the following questions with a partner or in a small group.

1. Which photos seem to be of works of art?

2. Which photos look as if they illustrate something about science or engineering?

3. What is origami? Have you ever done any paper folding?

B **Topic vocabulary.** The following words appear in Reading 2. Look at the words and answer the questions with a partner.

complex	insight	researcher
craft	inspired	sculpture
design	mathematical	technology
expression	model	telescope

1. Which words relate to art?

2. Which words relate to science or engineering?

3. Which words suggest the reading is about how we get new ideas?

C **Predict.** What do you think this reading will be about? Discuss each word in Exercise B and predict how it may relate to the reading.

Have you ever made paper birds, frogs, or boxes by folding paper? Read about some extraordinary new applications of origami—the traditional art of paper folding.

An origami horse created by physicist Robert Lang. Lang's theories of origami have many real-world applications.

ORIGAMI

The Practical Applications of a Familiar Art

ORIGAMI: THE PRACTICAL APPLICATIONS OF A FAMILIAR ART

One piece of paper, no cuts. Even in its simplest form, origami, the art of paper folding, has enchanted people for generations. As children, most of us have folded squares of paper to make boats, birds, and butterflies. Since the first instruction manual, *A Thousand Cranes*, was published in Japan in 1797, paper birds have landed on countless windowsills.[1] Since then, origami artists have elevated this form of expression from a hobby to a respected form of sculpture. The most famous origami master was the Japanese artist Akira Yoshizawa. His work has been exhibited in museums all over the world, including the Louvre in Paris.

These days, however, the ancient art is taking another form of expression: math. Origami experts can now describe their work mathematically and model it with computers. With these advances, they have moved from paper to metal and plastic and from craft to technology and science. The principles of origami are finding real-world applications. The value of origami is that it allows you to fold something large into a very small space. These tiny folded creations have already flown in space. Someday one may end up in one of your arteries.[2]

"It's now mathematically proven that you can pretty much fold anything," says Robert J. Lang. He quit his job as a physicist to fold things full-time. "We've basically solved how to create any appendage[3] or shape." In the 1990s, origami experts came to the realization that each appendage of a paper figure consists of a folded flap of paper. The flap is made from a circular section of the original square. This insight was crucial, Lang says, because it allowed origami experts to relate origami to a very old mathematical puzzle. They connected the folding process to a mathematical method for putting spheres into a box or circles into a square. This insight also allowed these artists to create complex creatures with numerous arms and legs as well as lively scenes such as musicians playing instruments. Perhaps more important, however, it led some of them to discover significant technological applications of paper

---

[1] *windowsills:* shelves along the bottom of a window

[2] *arteries:* blood vessels that carry blood from your heart to other parts of the body

[3] *appendage:* an arm, wing, or leg

Origami master Akira Yoshizawa displays some of his complex works of origami.

17-foot model of a telescope lens designed using principles of origami

folding. For example, engineers working on the design of car air bags asked Lang to figure out the best way to fold one into a small space. He realized that his design for origami insects would do the trick. "It was an unexpected solution," he says.

The car air bag is not the only practical application of origami. Lang has helped design a telescope lens that collapses like an umbrella. Only a five-foot model for this exists so far, but it unfolds to nearly 17 feet (about 5 meters). The plan is to create a telescope lens that will be the size of a football field but will fold down to just 10 feet (3 meters). In the medical field, researchers at Oxford University are working at the other size extreme. They are creating tiny origami stents[4] to support damaged arteries. These tiny tubes are only half an inch (12 millimeters) long when they are folded up. Once they are inside the artery, the stents expand to twice that size

—————————————

[4] *stents:* tiny tubes that are inserted into blood vessels to keep them open

(see Figure 1). The design of these devices is very much like the origami boxes that many children learn to fold.

Other projects are still in the development stage. A pair of researchers in Texas has designed a pad of paper that is inspired by origami. Health workers can use it as part of a blood test to diagnose diseases such as malaria even when they are far from a hospital. A drop of blood reacts with chemicals in the folded layers of paper to show if the patient has the disease. Scientists at Harvard University are working on designs for boxes made of self-folding DNA. They are billions of times smaller than a grain of rice and will be able to deliver drugs to diseased cells. 5

If we look to nature, we can see folding everywhere. Flowers, wings, mountain ranges, eyelids, and the structure of proteins all involve some sort of folding. So, it should come as no surprise that we can use this knowledge in emerging technology. "We haven't reached the limits of what origami can do," Lang says. "We 6

can't even see those limits." He believes it has the potential to improve our lives in many ways. He even believes that the applications of origami may one day save a life.

Figure 1. Stent Expanding in an Artery

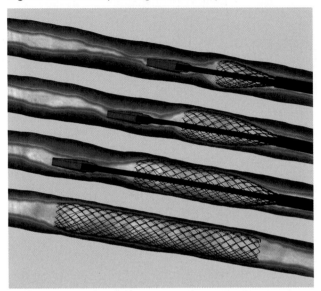

READING COMPREHENSION

Big Picture

Ⓐ The following statements are the main ideas of the first five paragraphs in Reading 2. Write the correct paragraph number next to its main idea.

_____ **1.** Many new applications are likely in the future.

_____ **2.** Origami has moved from an art form to high technology.

_____ **3.** The art of origami has a long history.

_____ **4.** Paper folding can be modeled mathematically.

_____ **5.** The principles of paper folding have been applied to practical problems.

Ⓑ Which statement in Exercise A best expresses the main idea of the *whole* reading? _____

Close-Up

Ⓐ Choose the best answer for each of the following questions according to Reading 2.

1. How have most people around the world become familiar with origami?
a. As a form of art you can find in museums
b. As a hobby
c. As a part of mathematics

2. What is special about origami that has potential applications for science and technology?
   a. It allows something large to fit somewhere small.
   b. It is found everywhere in nature.
   c. It follows basic principles of mathematics.

3. Which of Lang's origami designs helped him with the car air-bag project?
   a. Appendages from circles
   b. Spheres packed inside of boxes
   c. An insect with many legs

4. Which of the following statements is *not* true?
   a. Lang has created a telescope the size of a football field.
   b. Car air bags are folded using techniques from origami.
   c. Doctors have repaired arteries using small devices with designs based on origami.

5. Which medical application of origami is *not* mentioned in the reading?
   a. It can deliver medication to patients.
   b. It can repair broken bones.
   c. It can show whether a patient has an infection.

6. Reading 2 does *not* discuss applications of origami folding principles in which of the following fields?
   a. Chemistry   b. Engineering   c. Medicine

B With a partner, discuss which practical application of origami is likely to have the most impact. Give an explanation for your choice.

Reading Skill

Cohesion: Following Topic Chains

In academic texts, a topic may be mentioned several times. These repeated references to the same topic create cohesion, or connection between ideas. You may see the same word repeated, but there may also be other kinds of references to that same topic. They all help to create cohesive topic chains.

1. Personal pronouns and possessive forms (*he, it, they, their*)

   Kirigami is a variation of origami. However, it involves cutting as well as folding.

2. Other pronouns (*one, some*)

   The most popular kirigami form is the snowflake. You may have made one in school.

3. Synonyms or phrases that refer to the topic

   Kirigami involves both folding and cutting paper. However, this art form has never been as popular as origami.

4. Other signal words such as *this, these,* and *such* (see Unit 1, page 18). Remember that *this* can refer to a whole sentence and not just a single noun phrase.

   When you make a kirigami snowflake, you fold the paper in half and then in thirds. This creates a symmetrical pattern with six sections.

A Follow the steps below to find topic chains in the following section of paragraph 3 from Reading 2. You will look for repetition of words, a synonym or phrase that means the same thing, a pronoun, or another signal word.

1. Look for the topic chain about *origami experts*. Underline and number the four references.
2. Look for the topic chain about *this insight*. Circle and number the four references.

"It's now mathematically proven that you can pretty much fold anything," says Robert J. Lang. He quit his job as a physicist to fold things full-time. "We've basically solved how to create any appendage or shape." In the 1990s, origami experts *1* came to the realization that each appendage of a paper figure consists of a folded flap of paper. The flap is made from a circular section of the original square. This insight was crucial, Lang says, because it allowed origami experts to relate origami to a very old mathematical puzzle. They connected the folding process to a mathematical method for putting spheres into a box or circles into a square. This insight also allowed these artists to create complex creatures with numerous arms and legs as well as lively scenes such as musicians playing instruments. Perhaps more important, however, it led some of them to discover significant technological applications of paper folding.

Origami master Robert Lang at work in his studio

B Find three topic chains in paragraph 4 from Reading 2. Write them in the chart below. For each one, write the references that the writer uses to create cohesion. The first one is done for you.

Start of Topic	Topic Chain References
1. *telescope lens*	*this; it; telescope lens*
2.	
3.	

The car air bag is not the only practical application of origami. Lang has helped design a telescope lens that collapses like an umbrella. Only a five-foot model for this exists so far, but it unfolds to nearly 17 feet (about 5 meters). Eventually, the actual telescope lens will be the size of a football field but will fold down to just 10 feet (3 meters). In the medical field, researchers at Oxford University are working at the other size extreme. They are creating tiny origami stents to support damaged arteries (see Figure 1). These tiny tubes are only half an inch (12 millimeters) long when they are folded up. Once they are inside the artery, the stents expand to twice that size. The design of these devices is very much like the origami boxes that many children learn to fold.

C Compare your answers to Exercise B with a partner. What is the most common kind of reference used to create cohesion?

VOCABULARY PRACTICE

Academic Vocabulary

A Find the words in bold in Reading 2. Use the context to help you match sentence parts to create definitions.

_____ **1.** If you are **enchanted** (Par. 1) by something,

_____ **2.** A **manual** (Par. 1) is

_____ **3.** If you have **elevated** (Par. 1) something,

_____ **4.** If something has been **exhibited** (Par. 1),

_____ **5.** If you **quit** (Par. 3) something,

_____ **6.** **Spheres** (Par. 3) are

_____ **7.** A **lens** (Par. 4) is

_____ **8.** When you **diagnose** (Par. 5) something,

a. solid balls.

b. you recognize a disease or problem as the result of examination and study.

c. you have moved it to a higher or more important level.

d. a piece of glass with a curved surface that makes objects appear larger.

e. it has been shown in a public place.

f. you stop doing it or being part of it.

g. a book of instructions on how to use something.

h. you find it very attractive.

B Choose an academic word from Exercise A to complete each of the following sentences. Notice and learn the words in bold because they often appear with the academic words. In some cases, you need to change the verb or noun form.

1. The doctor was able to _____ the man's **illness** immediately.

2. The museum visitors were **completely** _____ by the room filled with tiny dollhouses.

3. Earth is not a **perfect** _____. It is slightly flat at the poles.

4. The two students borrowed a special **camera** _____ for their art project.

5. The new art museum has _____ the **level** of culture in the city.

6. I have lost the **instruction** _____ for my computer so I cannot fix it.

7. After a serious disagreement with his manager, he decided to _____ his **job**.

8. These **paintings** have been _____ at art galleries all over the world.

Multiword Vocabulary

A Find the words in bold in Reading 2. Then write the words that come before and/or after them to complete the multiword vocabulary.

1. _____ **days** (Par. 2)

2. _____ **up** (Par. 2)

3. **came to** _____ _____ **that** (Par. 3)

4. **do the** _____ (Par. 3)

5. **practical** _____ (Par. 4)

6. _____ **of paper** (Par. 5)

7. **some** _____ **of** (Par. 6)

8. **has the** _____ (Par. 6)

B Complete the following sentences with the correct multiword vocabulary from Exercise A. Use the information in parentheses to help you. In some cases, you need to change the verb form.

1. A lot more people are using public transportation to get to work _____ (recently and frequently).

2. The discovery of a large deposit of oil _____ (introduces the possibility) reduce the price of many oil-based products such as gasoline.

3. After working in several low-paying jobs, he _____ (began to understand) he would have to go back to school to improve his skills.

4. All of the visitors received a(n) _____ (a large number of sheets fastened together) so they could write down their ideas and reactions.

5. The lock was easy to open even without a key. A paper clip _____ (was just the right solution) and we were inside in a few minutes.

6. After driving for five hours, we _____ (eventually arrived) at a small town by the sea.

7. Several archaeologists have examined the object, but they cannot figure out what it is. They think it is _____ (a type of) tool.

8. Often when scientists make a discovery, it is not clear right away what its _____ (real-world use) will be.

Use the Vocabulary

Write answers to the following questions. Use the words in bold in your answers. Then share your answers with a partner.

1. When you get a new piece of equipment, are you the kind of person who likes to figure out how to use it by yourself, or do you use the **instruction manual**? If you do it yourself, do you ever **come to the realization that** you need to read the manual after all?

2. Governments often provide money for scientific research. Some people believe that they should only fund research that **has the potential** for **practical applications**. Others say that it is too hard to say which research will **end up** being useful and that the government should provide support for all kinds of science. What is your view?

3. Some people complain that **these days** young people will **quit** an activity if it is too hard. Do you think this is true? Do you think it is/was true for you? Explain your answer.

4. Have you ever been **enchanted** by a movie, play, or piece of art? Describe it.

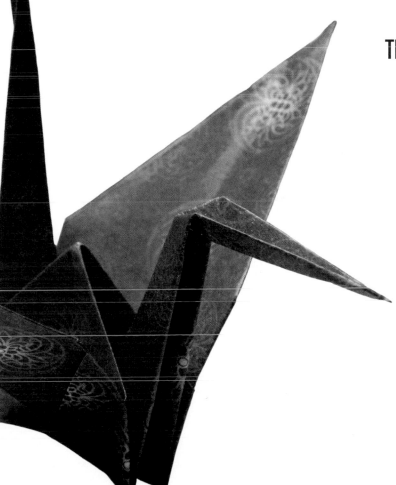

THINK AND DISCUSS

Work in a small group. Use the information in the reading and your own ideas to discuss the following questions.

1. **Summarize.** According to Reading 2, why is origami important beyond its beauty as an art form?

2. **Relate to personal experience.** When you do paper folding or other forms of art, do you ever think about it in terms of math or practical applications? Explain your answer.

3. **Making connections.** Reading 2 says that folding is everywhere. Where can you find things that are folded?

4. **Expressing an opinion.** What do you think of someone who quits a job to pursue a passion? Do you know anyone who has done this? Would you?

Vocabulary Review

A Complete the reading with the vocabulary below that you have studied in the unit.

at the height of its power	from far and wide	laid the foundation for	practical applications
elevate the level	key components	made a mark	sustained the growth
ended up	it comes as no surprise that		

The Song Dynasty (960–1280 CE) was an exciting period in Chinese history.

_____, the country's population doubled. A prosperous economy and support
          1

from Chinese rulers _____ of technology and the expansion of knowledge.
          2

During this period, a huge number of technological innovations emerged. Many of them had

significant _____.
          3

One particular invention from this period _____ on the world: moveable
          4

type—that is, moveable blocks that could print a single letter and then be used again. The first

moveable type was made from blocks of clay in the 11th century, but later printers used wooden and

metal blocks. This technology finally _____ in Europe several centuries later.
          5

The Chinese language uses a huge number of characters, but most European languages use an

alphabet. Printing texts in an alphabet requires fewer blocks. This invention

_____ a revolution in written communication in Europe and helped
          6

_____ of literacy there. Increasingly, even less educated people were able to read.
          7

The Chinese were also the first to discover the _____ of gunpowder, the
          8

explosive material that is used in guns and other weapons. _____ that rulers
          9

_____ were eager to start using this new compound. As a result, this innovation
          10

quickly spread around the ancient world.

B Compare answers to Exercise A with a partner. Then discuss the following question.

Compare the impacts of moveable type and gunpowder. Which impact has been greater?

C Complete the following sentences in a way that shows that you understand the
meaning of the words in bold.

1. The children were **completely enchanted** by _____.

2. I have finally **come to the realization that** _____.

3. Alternative energy such as solar and wind **have the potential** to _____.

4. I **quit my job** because _____.

D Work with a partner and write sentences that include any six of the vocabulary items
below. You may use any verb tense and make nouns plural if you wish.

at the heart of	draw on	pad of paper	tackle the problem
chemical compound	instruction manual	some sort of	these days
do the trick	massive amount		

A master craftsman demonstrates traditional techniques of Chinese printing at a book fair in Germany.

Connect the Readings

A Look back at Readings 1 and 2, and fill in the chart with the practical applications mentioned in the reading.

Technique	Practical Applications in Reading 1 or 2
Distillation	
Paper folding	

B With a partner or in a small group, compare your answers to Exercise A. Then discuss the following questions.

1. What do you think the goal of the Islamic chemists was when they invented distillation?

2. Do you think origami experts have had similar goals to those of Islamic chemists? Why, or why not?

3. In what ways were the invention processes different in these two cases?

4. What additional innovations did you list? Which innovations play a part in your daily life?

C Discuss the following questions with a partner. Use your understanding of the readings and your own ideas.

1. The two readings discuss two invention processes. One involves intentional discovery; the other involves the practical application of a technique that originally had a very different purpose. Can you think of any other examples of inventions or discoveries that were the result of either of these two kinds of processes?

2. Some important discoveries and inventions have occurred completely by accident. Do you know of any like this? If so, describe them to your partner.

People watch robots dancing during
a trade show in Beijing, China.

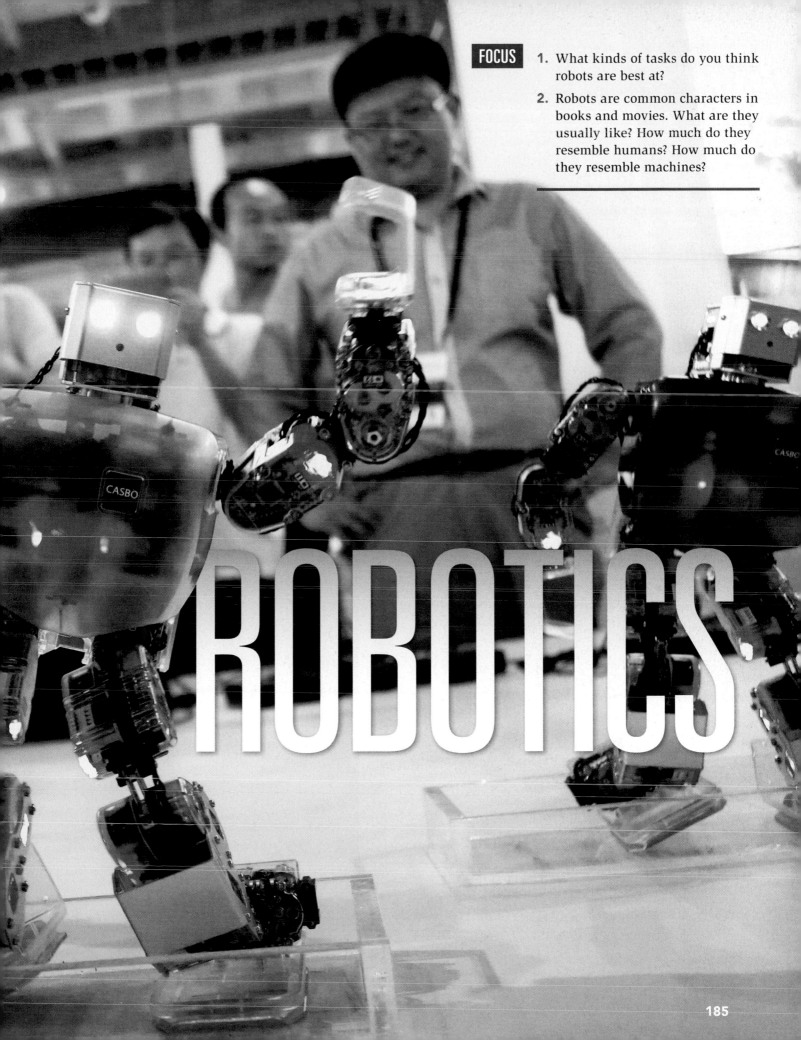

1. What kinds of tasks do you think robots are best at?

2. Robots are common characters in books and movies. What are they usually like? How much do they resemble humans? How much do they resemble machines?

ROBOTICS

Academic Vocabulary

to defuse	to exhale	remote
desperately	to inspect	to scan
to detect	oblivious	

Multiword Vocabulary

to be on the safe side	from a vantage point
a close call	a hazardous material
to come to the rescue	out of harm's way
a false alarm	to rest on the shoulders of

Reading Preview

A **Preview.** Read the first sentence of each of the paragraphs in the boxes on pages 188–190 and look at the photos. Then discuss the following questions with a partner or in a small group.

1. What sorts of situations will be described in the reading?

2. What do the photos show?

3. How do you think robots could help in these situations?

B **Topic vocabulary.** The following words appear in Reading 1. Look at the words and answer the questions with a partner.

bombs	hazardous	survivors
earthquake	rescue	toxic
explosives	search	trapped
firefighters	soldiers	wounded

1. What words are related to natural disasters or other dangerous situations?

2. Which words refer to people who can help when you are in danger?

3. Which words are positive or hopeful?

C **Predict.** What do you think this reading will be about? Discuss each word in Exercise B and predict how it may relate to the reading.

There have been tremendous advances in the world of robotics—the design and operation of robots. The latest robots can help people in all kinds of dangerous situations!

Robots
to the Rescue

ROBOTS TO THE RESCUE

When you picture a robot, you may think of the ones in movies or cartoons. However, most real robots don't serve coffee or blow up spaceships. Instead, many of today's robots are helping to keep people out of harm's way. They do skilled work in dangerous situations, which, in the past, had to be done by humans. In the future, these responsibilities will increasingly rest on the shoulders of robots.

A railroad car carrying poisonous chemicals goes off the tracks in a remote location in the woods. A few minutes later, it explodes into a fire so hot that firefighters cannot get near it. A cloud of toxic gas rises above the fire, making it difficult to breathe. The firefighters come within 300 feet (90 meters) of the fire and then send in a robot. The robot rolls in close to the fire, oblivious to the extreme heat and toxic gas, and shoots water from two hoses. The firefighters watch from a vantage point behind the trees. Within 40 minutes, the fire is out. Everyone is safe, but it was a close call.

A woman calls the police about a suspicious   3
package in the hallway near her office. The police
are concerned it could be dangerous, perhaps
even a bomb. They tell everyone to leave the
building and then send in a robot the size of a
small vacuum cleaner.[1] The robot approaches the
package and checks for the presence of any chemicals that might cause an explosion. It detects
nothing, but it is better to be on the safe side. The
robot sticks out its mechanical arms
and picks up the package, carries it
outside to an empty parking lot, and
destroys it. The police inspect what
remains of the package. Fortunately, it
turns out to be a false alarm. It was just
somebody's lunch!

---

[1] *vacuum cleaner:* a machine used for cleaning up
   the dirt on floors and carpets

Soldiers are moving through enemy territory.   4
Suddenly, half a mile away, their commanding
officer hears gunfire. He is worried. Are his
soldiers safe? Are any of them wounded? The
commander wants to rescue them, but he doesn't
want to risk the life of another soldier. So, he
sends in his rescue robot. It moves quickly across
the rough terrain. As it detects the shape of a
human body, it moves closer. When it is within
200 feet (60 meters) of the body on the ground, it
turns its camera toward the face. It scans the face
and checks the image against all of the photos of
soldiers that are stored in its internal computer.
Yes, it is one of the soldiers! The robot lifts the
wounded soldier in its "arms" and carries him
back to safety. The soldier is alive but badly hurt.
The robot has saved his life.

It has been three days since the terrible earthquake that caused buildings all over the city to collapse. The search-and-rescue teams are trying desperately to find survivors, but most buildings are so unstable that it is not safe to go inside them. Rescuers call out and knock on walls, but they cannot hear any voices. If there are survivors inside, they will be thirsty, hungry, and perhaps badly injured, but the rescuers are helpless. Will anyone come to the rescue? Here come the robot cockroaches![1] Scientists have attached tiny computer chips to live cockroaches and turned them into tiny robots. The search-and-rescue team have sent the cockroaches into a collapsed building to search for signs of life. The cockroaches can detect heat from a living body and the carbon dioxide that humans exhale.

5

[1] *cockroach:* a large, flat, black or brown insect that often lives in the same environments as humans

They also carry tiny cameras that send back images to the team. Forty minutes later, a signal comes back from one of the cockroach robots—someone is alive! Slowly, emergency workers remove bricks and stones until they find the survivor—an-eleven-year-old boy who was trapped under a collapsed wall.

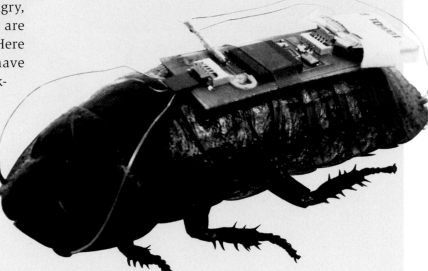

Is this science fiction or are these stories true? The first two stories describe situations that are already a reality. Robots are being used in situations that involve hazardous materials, and they are programmed to check for bombs. Robots were used in the Fukushima Daiichi nuclear reactor[1] after it was damaged in an earthquake and tsunami in Japan in 2011. The release of radioactive material made conditions in the reactor too dangerous for workers. Robots took pictures and measured radiation and temperature levels. This information helped officials make important safety decisions. The military regularly uses robots to defuse bombs, a job that used to fall to explosives experts. In the past, some explosives experts died doing their jobs, but today they no longer have to take such risks.

6

The second two stories may take place in the future, but new technology is bringing that future closer every day. Engineers are developing robots that can travel quickly for miles across

7

[1] *nuclear reactor:* a very large device that produces nuclear energy

rough terrain. They can pick up objects, send information to remote locations, and even recognize faces. Developers hope to test them in real situations soon. The story of the wounded soldier describes a military use for robots, but there are many non-military search-and-rescue situations where these robots would be helpful.

The final story illustrates a new type of robot. Scientists are developing *biobots* that combine the advanced technology of robotics with the advantages of real animals. The developers of the cockroach biobots say that they are superior to fully robotic devices. The cockroaches' natural abilities allow them to move around and survive almost anywhere. In search-and-rescue operations, engineers use the computer chip to control them wirelessly, directing where and when they move. Developers of these biobots hope their work will soon be ready to help people who are in life-threatening situations.

8

Robots have many uses—in factories, in medicine, in homes. But perhaps their most important job is to help people in dangerous situations.

9

READING COMPREHENSION

Big Picture

A Read the functions of paragraphs in the first column. Check (✓) the paragraphs that have each function. Some paragraphs may have more than one function.

Functions of the Paragraph	Paragraph Number						
	2	3	4	5	6	7	8
1. Describes and explains the abilities of today's robots							
2. Describes and explains the potential abilities of robots of the future							
3. Gives example(s) of dangerous situations in which robots could be useful							
4. Gives example(s) of situations in which robots provide information from a remote location							
5. Describes situation(s) in which robots could help rescue people who are injured							

B Compare answers to Exercise A with a partner. How is the function of the paragraphs in boxes different from the function of the paragraphs in the second half of the reading?

Close-Up

A Complete the following sentences about Reading 1 in your own words.

1. Robots can help protect the safety of the public by _____.

2. The robot in the second story picked up the package and _____.

3. The robot in the third story knew it had located a soldier because _____.

4. The biobot in the fourth story knew the boy was alive because _____.

5. The _____ and _____ stories were based on facts.

6. The robot in the Fukushima Daiichi nuclear plant _____.

B Compare your answers to Exercise A with a partner. Discuss any differences.

Reading Skill

Ⓐ Read the paragraph below from Reading 1. Then underline information that answers each of the following questions.

1. Why are biobots especially useful? (main idea question)

2. What is an example of a situation in which the use of biobots would be an effective strategy? (supporting detail question)

   The final story illustrates a new type of robot. Scientists are developing *biobots* that combine the advanced technology of robotics with the advantages of real animals. The developers of the cockroach biobots say that they are superior to fully robotic devices. The cockroaches' natural abilities allow them to move around and survive almost anywhere. In search-and-rescue operations, engineers use the computer chip to control them wirelessly, directing where and when they move. Developers of these biobots hope their work will soon be ready to help people who are in life-threatening situations.

Ⓑ Work with a partner.

1. Choose two more paragraphs from Reading 1. Write two questions for each:
      • A main idea question
      • A supporting detail question

2. Exchange questions with your partner. Underline the information in the reading that answers his or her questions.

VOCABULARY PRACTICE

Academic Vocabulary

A Find the words in bold in Reading 1. Use the context to help you choose the definition that is closest to the meaning in the reading.

1. **oblivious** (Par. 2)   a. paying no attention   b. showing concern

2. **detects** (Par. 3)   a. understands   b. notices

3. **inspect** (Par. 3)   a. throw away   b. examine

4. **scans** (Par. 4)   a. studies   b. looks quickly

5. **desperately** (Par. 5)   a. urgently   b. carefully

6. **exhale** (Par. 5)   a. breathe out   b. consume

7. **defuse** (Par. 6)   a. explode   b. make less dangerous

8. **remote** (Par. 7)   a. safe   b. distant

B Work with a partner to choose the best word to complete each of the following sentences. Give reasons for your choices. Notice and learn the words in the box because they often appear with the academic words.

carefully	crowd	locations	situation
changes	hoping	quickly	totally

1. Thousands of students are **desperately** _____ that they will be accepted into a top university.

2. The students continued working on their projects and were _____ **oblivious** to the loud noises outside of the classroom window.

3. The new machines are very sensitive, so they can **detect** even very small _____ that have occurred in the environment.

4. Officials at the border **inspected** all of the suitcases very _____. They were checking for explosives and other illegal material. It took a long time.

5. The crowd grew angry and everyone was very tense, but then the president began to speak quietly. This quickly **defused** a _____ that might have become dangerous.

6. The new technology allows the doctors at the main hospital to communicate with doctors and nurses in **remote** _____.

7. During the scary part of the movie, I held my breath and then _____ **exhaled** when the danger was over.

8. He **scanned** the _____ to see if his friends had already arrived at the football game.

Multiword Vocabulary

A Find the multiword vocabulary in bold in Reading 1 and use the context to help you understand the meaning. Then match each item to the correct definition.

_____ 1. **out of harm's way** (Par. 1)

_____ 2. **rest on the shoulders of** (Par. 1)

_____ 3. **from a vantage point** (Par. 2)

_____ 4. **a close call** (Par. 2)

_____ 5. **be on the safe side** (Par. 3)

_____ 6. **a false alarm** (Par. 3)

_____ 7. **come to the rescue** (Par. 5)

_____ 8. **hazardous materials** (Par. 6)

a. be someone's sole responsibility because others cannot take it

b. a warning or signal about an emergency when there is no real emergency

c. safe; away from danger

d. save someone or something from danger or failure

e. something bad that almost happens

f. dangerous substances

g. do something extra in order to prepare for something bad that might happen

h. from a position from which you can observe things

B Complete the following sentences using the multiword vocabulary from Exercise A. Use the information in parentheses to help you. In some cases, you need to change the word form.

1. The car engine is making very strange noises. Let's get it checked at the repair shop just to _____ (be prepared for anything that might happen).

2. After his illness, the success of the family business _____ (was their responsibility) his two daughters.

3. The soldiers could watch the enemy _____ (from a place where they can see all around) at the top of the mountain.

4. _____ (harmful chemicals) spilled all over the highway when two trucks crashed. The police had to close down the road for several hours until it was cleaned up.

5. The two planes came within one kilometer of each other. There was no accident, but it was _____ (almost a very bad situation).

6. The mother lion hid her babies in a cave, where they were _____ (safe from enemies).

7. In many fairy tales, a handsome prince _____ (help out of a difficult or dangerous situation) of a beautiful princess who is in trouble.

8. Someone reported that a burglar was in the building, but, in fact, no one was there. Thankfully, it was just _____ (a situation that everyone thought was bad but was not).

Use the Vocabulary

Write answers to the following questions. Use the words in bold in your answers. Then share your answers with a partner.

1. Have you ever been in a dangerous situation in which you had **a close call**, for example, when you almost had a bad accident? What would you do in the future to prevent it from happening again, just to **be on the safe side**?

2. Many countries have taken steps to increase security on their borders. There are dogs in airports that can **detect** the smell of food, drugs, or **hazardous materials**. Special machines **scan** fingerprints and faces to find visitors who might be dangerous. Officials carefully **inspect** all luggage. Do you think these steps are necessary to protect us or do they violate our privacy? Explain your answer.

3. Imagine you are a police officer in a roomful of angry people. It seems that there is the potential for violence to break out. The responsibility for keeping everything peaceful **rests on the shoulders of** the police. What steps would you take to **defuse** this tense situation?

4. There are two kinds of stories in popular culture about what happens if you **come to the rescue** and save a person's life. One idea is that person is in your debt for the rest of his or her life and must help you whenever you are in trouble. A second idea is the opposite. You have saved a life once and you now become responsible for that life forever. Do you agree with either idea? If so, which one? Give reasons for your answer.

THINK AND DISCUSS

Work in a small group. Use the information in the reading and your own ideas to discuss the following questions.

1. **Evaluate.** What do you think are the limits on robots' abilities? In other words, what do you think they will never be able to do?

2. **Express an opinion.** The reading describes cockroach biobots. What do you think about biobots with more advanced animals? Would you be in favor of that?

3. **Compare.** Are there any possible negative consequences of using robots in dangerous situations? What about in wars?

4. **Apply knowledge.** Reading 1 addresses robots in dangerous situations. Where else do you think robots can be useful and effective?

Academic Vocabulary

to approximate	to mimic	to protest
an aspiration	miniature	a version
convincing	a paradox	

Multiword Vocabulary

to be after something	a long way to go
to cross the line	a measure of success
from head to toe	to put something to the test
a key feature	to spend one's life

Reading Preview

A **Preview.** Read the subheadings in Reading 2. Look at the photos and read their captions. Then discuss the following questions with a partner or in a small group.

1. Do these robots look like robots you have seen before or that you have imagined?

2. What seems different about these robots, if anything?

3. How close do you think robots can get to humans in their appearance and behavior?

B **Topic vocabulary.** The following words appear in Reading 2. Look at the words and answer the questions with a partner.

expressive	model	resemble
gesture	observe	respond
identical	react	similar
interact	recognize	scowl

1. Which words do you associate more with human abilities and behavior than with robots?

2. Which verbs are related to communicating?

3. Which words are connected to things that are the same or almost the same?

C **Predict.** What do you think this reading will be about? Discuss each word in Exercise B and predict how it may relate to the reading.

Scientists and engineers are trying to design robots that are just like human beings. How close will they come to their goal? How close do we want them to come?

A humanoid robot called "Robo Thespian" at the Carnegie Science Museum robot exhibit in Pittsburgh, Pennsylvania, USA

Humanoids

Hiroshi Ishiguro with
humanoid newscaster

Robots in science fiction movies and books   1
are often evil figures that try to take over
our world. When you enter Professor
Hiroshi Ishiguro's laboratory at ATR Intelligent
Robotics and Communication Laboratories in
Kyoto, Japan, you might think you are in one
of those movies. He has spent his professional
life building robots. His goal has been to create
a robot that is as similar as possible to a real
human being. Such robots are called *humanoids*.

Ishiguro's most famous humanoid creation is   2
his own robotic twin. At ATR, the two of them
are dressed from head to toe in black. The robot
sits in a chair behind Ishiguro, with identical
black hair and a thoughtful scowl. Like others
working in human-robot-interaction research,
Ishiguro is not just interested in technology.
He is after something much more exciting. He
wants to reveal what is fundamentally human by
creating increasingly accurate approximations of
ourselves. Ishiguro observes how we react to the
robots. Then he uses those responses to create
new models that are even more convincing. "You
believe I'm real, and you believe that thing is not
human," he says, gesturing back at his twin. "But
this distinction will become more difficult as the
technology advances."

Creating Humanoids

There are many challenges in creating   3
robots that resemble humans. Robotics experts
must design machines that are physically similar to humans, both in their appearance and
movements. These pioneers have even higher
aspirations, however. They want to create
humanoids that behave, learn, and think like

humans and relate to us in familiar ways. These robots need to be able to recognize key features in an unpredictable environment—such as human voice, movements, and expressions—and then perform a variety of tasks in response.

Scientists and engineers have 4 used a range of advanced technology to improve their models. One model is the Telenoid, a small robot that allows complex interaction through cellular phones. Motion-capture technology[1] senses the movements of your face and body, which are transmitted, along with your voice, through a cellular phone to the Telenoid. The Telenoid then mimics all of these movements and facial expressions for a person on the other end of the phone. Ishiguro and his colleagues are working on a tiny version of the

> *"Soon, your friends will be able to hold a miniature, but fully expressive, version of you in their hands during your conversation…"*

[1] *motion-capture technology:* a method for digitally recording the movements of people or things. It is frequently used in making movies.

Telenoid. The Elfoid is the size of very small baby and, like the Telenoid, it receives and transmits these signals. Soon, your friends will be able to hold a miniature, but fully expressive, version of you in their hands during your conversation, even when the real you is in a remote location.

How Close Is Too Close?

Some robotics experts report 5 an apparent paradox in their work. They are trying to create robots that closely approximate human appearance and behavior, but is it possible for their creations to be too good? Could the robots be too human? Studies show that people prefer robots that are clearly robots. If the robots' physical appearance or behavior comes too close to human, people become uncomfortable. Interacting with humanoids that seem truly human can feel strange, even frightening—like science fiction. Some experts say they do not want to cross that line with their models.

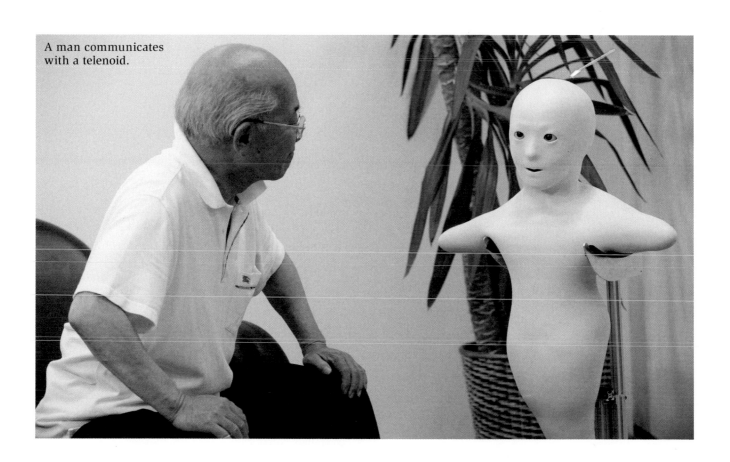

A man communicates with a telenoid.

Other experts say the most important measure of success in creating humanoids is not how much they look and act like humans. It is how we respond to them. For example, do we believe their existence has a value, similar to a human life? One scientist, Peter Kahn, decided to put this idea to the test. He asked children and adolescents to play games with a cute little humanoid named Robovie. He interrupted the game when Robovie was about to take his turn. He told the robot it was time to put him away in the closet. Robovie protested that this was unfair. "You're just a robot. It doesn't matter," the scientist answered. More than half the human players agreed that it was unfair to put Robovie away in the closet. According to Kahn, this is an indication that they had begun to think that Robovie, like human beings, has moral value. 6

The field of robotics has a long way to go before we have to worry about robots taking over our world. Every year, however, scientists like Ishiguro make the line between humanoid and human harder to distinguish. 7

Robovie

READING COMPREHENSION

Big Picture

A Choose the best answer for each of the following questions.

1. What is the main idea of paragraph 2?
   a. Ishiguro believes that humanoids can reveal what being human really means.
   b. Ishiguro believes he can make humanoids that look just like humans.

2. What is the main idea of paragraph 3?
   a. Robotics researchers have made a lot of progress in developing robots that are more like humans.
   b. Designing humanoids involves much more than creating a robot that looks and moves like a human being.

3. What is the main idea of paragraph 4?
   a. Robotics experts have created robots that can use the telephone.
   b. Robotics experts have incorporated emerging technology into their work.

4. What is the main idea of paragraph 5?
   a. People don't like it when robots are too human.
   b. People don't like to interact with humanoids.

5. What is the purpose of paragraph 6?
   a. It gives the results of a study about robots.
   b. It shows that it is possible for people to believe that robots have feelings.

B Write a sentence that expresses the main idea of the *whole* reading.

_____

Close-Up

A List five characteristics that designers hope to include in their humanoid robots. These are the characteristics that make the robots seem human.

1. _____
2. _____
3. _____
4. _____
5. _____

B List two ways in which humans respond to humanoids that seem very close to human.

1. _____
2. _____

Reading Skill

Active Reading

Active readers constantly ask themselves questions. They use their questions to make predictions about what will come next. Fluent readers do this smoothly as part of their reading process. It is more difficult to do in a second language in a text where some of the words are unfamiliar. You can still be an active reader; however, you may have to read more slowly and carefully.

1. Use cues such as *first*, *second*, *however*, *therefore*, *many*, *some*, and *this* to help you read actively. When you read one of these cues, ask yourself questions about what will come next and what came before.

2. Make predictions based on your questions. Check your predictions as you read.

3. Use your questions to help you catch details that you may have missed before.

Examples

Robots are used in many different settings.

   Ask yourself: What are those settings? Will the text tell me? Scan ahead to find out.

The first design challenge is . . .

   Predict: There must be at least one more challenge later in the text.

All of these are important factors.

   Catch up: *These* must refer to something earlier in the text. What does *these* refer to? Did I miss that?

A Reread paragraph 3 of Reading 2. Then fill out the chart that follows. The first example has been done for you. Note that the text may not always answer your questions.

There are many challenges in creating robots that resemble humans. Robotics experts must design machines that are physically similar to humans, both in their appearance and movements. These pioneers have even higher aspirations, however. They want to create humanoids that behave, learn, and think like humans and relate to us in familiar ways. These robots need to be able recognize key features in an unpredictable environment—such as human voice, movements, and expressions— and then perform a variety of tasks in response.

Cue	Action	Response
many challenges	Ask: What are they? Scan to find them.	*One challenge is to design robots that are like humans in appearance and movement.*
higher aspirations	Ask: Higher than what? Review prior text. Ask: What are they? Will the text tell me?	
key features	Ask: What are they?	
a variety of tasks	Ask: What are they? Will the text tell me?	

B Reread paragraphs 4, 5, and 6 in Reading 2. For each paragraph, find at least one cue that helped you to be an active reader. Fill out the chart as you did in Exercise A.

P#	Cue	Action	Response
4			
5			
6			

VOCABULARY PRACTICE

Academic Vocabulary

A Find the words in the box below in Reading 2. Use the context to help you choose the correct word to complete each of the following sentences. Use the information in parentheses to help you.

convincing (Par. 2)	mimics (Par. 4)	version (Par. 4)	approximate (Par. 5)
aspirations (Par. 3)	miniature (Par. 4)	paradox (Par. 5)	protested (Par. 6)

1. There is a monkey at the zoo that often _____ (copies) the movements of the human zoo visitors.

2. All of the students in the school have _____ (hopes) to attend top universities.

3. A new _____ (slightly different form) of the software has just been released. We will all have to update our computers.

4. The museum had a room full of _____ (very small) models of airplanes from the last century.

5. Scientists have provided _____ (persuasive) evidence of the genetic basis of some behavior.

6. The students _____ (expressed opposition) against the increase in educational costs.

7. It is a(n) _____ (inconsistency; puzzle) that there are so many poor people in the richest country in the world.

8. The model will _____ (be similar but not the exactly the same) what the city looked like 200 years ago.

B Work with a partner and discuss which words in the first column may frequently be found with the words in the second column. Match the words.

_____ 1. have high   **a.** approximate

_____ 2. an apparent   **b.** evidence

_____ 3. closely   **c.** aspirations

_____ 4. **protest**   **d.** the behavior

_____ 5. **mimic**   **e.** paradox

_____ 6. have **convincing**   **f.** against

C Choose a phrase from Exercise B to complete each of the following sentences.

1. Citizens marched in the streets to _____ the recent tax increase.

2. Engineers programmed the computer to _____ of human chess players.

3. Police say they _____ that the mayor had stolen money from the city.

4. Her mother always told her to _____. She might even become president!

5. Using the new recipe, I was able to _____ the cookies my grandmother used to make.

6. In _____, the government is starting new education programs at the same time that it is firing 10 percent of all teachers.

Multiword Vocabulary

A Find the multiword vocabulary in bold in Reading 2 and use the context to help you understand the meaning. Then match each item to the correct definition.

_____	**1. spent** his **life** (Par. 1)	**a.** do something that is inappropriate
_____	**2. from head to toe** (Par. 2)	**b.** considerable progress that is required before it will be ready.
_____	**3. is after** something (Par. 2)	
_____	**4. key features** (Par. 3)	**c.** primary or major characteristics
_____	**5. cross** that **line** (Par. 5)	**d.** gave all of his time
_____	**6. a measure of success** (Par. 6)	**e.** try something out to see if it works
_____	**7. put** this idea **to the test** (Par. 6)	**f.** over the entire body
_____	**8. a long way to go** (Par. 7)	**g.** try to get or succeed at something
		h. a modest, but not high, level of accomplishment

B Complete the following sentences using the multiword vocabulary from Exercise A. In some cases, you need to change the word form.

1. After playing in the rain, the little boys were covered _____ with mud.

2. Scientists have been working on the design for the rocket for many years. Today is the day to

_____.

3. Five years ago, the government began several programs to increase the educational level of the population. They have achieved _____, but more progress is still needed.

4. Bill Gates has _____ building his software company, Microsoft.

5. Some people want to make a lot of money, whereas other people

_____ power and fame.

6. It is fine to have disagreements, but insulting someone's family really

_____.

7. We have only finished 10 percent of the project, so we still have

_____.

8. The two _____ of the government's economic plan are lower interest rates and a program to increase jobs.

Use the Vocabulary

Write answers to the following questions. Use the words in bold in your answers. Then share your answers with a partner.

1. Have you ever been in a situation when you **were after something** that you wanted really badly, so badly that you **crossed the line**? What happened?

2. Early adopters are the people who want the newest **version** of everything from computers to cameras. They want to **put** new technology **to the test**. Then come the majority. Last come the people who lag behind. They **protest against** anything that is new. Which group are you in? Explain why.

3. What **key features** do you look for when you make a major purchase such as a car or computer?

4. What are your educational and professional **aspirations**? Name one area in which you have achieved **a measure of success**. Name another in which you still **have a long way to go**.

THINK AND DISCUSS

Work in a small group. Use the information in the reading and your own ideas to discuss the following questions.

1. **Express an opinion.** Does the idea of robots that act and look like humans make you uncomfortable? Explain your answer.

2. **Analyze.** Can machines such as robots ever have the same value as a human life? Why, or why not?

3. **Apply knowledge.** Do you think that there are any situations in which humanoids could present a danger to people?

4. **Use prior knowledge.** Think about robots you have seen in films or on television, or have read about in books. Why do you think we are fascinated with robots?

A scene from Karel Čapek's
play R.U.R., performed in
Berlin, Germany in 1923

Vocabulary Review

A Complete the reading with the vocabulary below that you have studied in the unit.

apparent paradox	cross the line	key feature	protest against
a close call	detect changes	mimic the behavior	rests on the shoulders of
comes to the rescue	higher aspirations		

   Czech playwright Karel Čapek invented the word *robot*. It first appeared in a play he wrote in 1921. The word is based on the Czech word for *work*. In the play, the robots are produced in a factory and their job is to work for humans and to make their lives easier. Čapek's robots were able to _____ and appearance of the humans in the play. They begin as quiet

   ₁

helpers who follow orders, but soon the audience begins to _____ in their

   ₂

behavior. These changes start when a scientist in the factory decides to give the robots emotions. Then they begin to develop _____, and they _____ their

   ₃   ₄

low position in society. Eventually, they _____. They begin to kill the humans

   ₅

and they take over the world.

   A(n) _____ of many fictional robots is that they reflect both the good and

   ₆

bad in humans. Some are helpful servants. Others are evil and threaten to destroy the human world. In a(n) _____, some reflect both of these. During the 1950s and 1960s,

   ₇

at the height of the Cold War, robot movies were particularly popular. In these movies, frequently the fate of the world _____ the human hero when robots try to take over. By

   ₈

the end, however, the hero always _____ of the human race. But it is usually

   ₉

_____!

   ₁₀

B Compare answers to Exercise A with a partner. Then discuss the following question.

   What ideas do you think Čapek was trying to convey in his play?

C Complete the following sentences in a way that shows that you understand the meaning of the words in bold.

1. There is **convincing evidence** that _____.

2. Everyone thought that _____, but it turned out to be just **a false alarm**.

3. _____ is considered a **hazardous material**.

4. Just to **be on the safe side**, you should always _____.

D Work with a partner and write sentences that include any six of the vocabulary items below. You may use any verb tense and make nouns plural if you wish.

closely approximate	from head to toe	out of harm's way	spend one's life
defuse a situation	a long way to go	remote location	totally oblivious
desperately hoping	measure of success		

Connect the Readings

A Look back at Readings 1 and 2. The robots in the two readings share some features, but they are also different in many ways. Fill in characteristics in the chart below.

	Robots in Reading 1	Robots in Reading 2
Approximation to human form and behavior		
Functions		
Designers' goals in creating them		
Potential for future benefit to humans		

B With a partner or in a small group, compare your answers to Exercise A. Then discuss the following questions.

1. How important do you think it is for robots to approximate human appearance and behavior?

2. Governments and private foundations often provide money for scientific research. What kind of robotics research do you think should get funding? Explain your answer.

C Discuss the following questions with a partner. Use your understanding of the readings and your own ideas.

1. Robots are becoming an increasingly normal part of our lives. Where are robots found in your community? (Consider all robots, not just the ones that look like humans.)

2. In what situations have robots already replaced humans? What have the results been?

3. Why do you think fictional accounts, such as the Čapek play (page 206), often show robots as a threat to humans?

VOCABULARY INDEX

The following words and phrases are studied in *Reading and Vocabulary Focus 3*. Each vocabulary item is listed according to which unit and reading it appears in. For example, a word or phrase listed as U1 R1 appears in the first reading of unit 1. If a word is in the Academic Word List, it is listed as AWL.

a breath of fresh air   U6 R1
a close call   U9 R1
a fact of life   U6 R1
a false alarm   U9 R1
a long way to go   U9 R2
a matter of life and death   U6 R1
a measure of success   U9 R2
a source of pride   U5 R1
a win-win situation   U5 R1
accelerate (*v*)   U5 R2
acknowledge (*v*) AWL   U5 R1
advantageous (*adj*)   U5 R1
affectionate (*adj*)   U5 R2
after all   U7 R2
aftermath (*n*)   U4 R2
aggressive (*adj*)   U5 R1
alarming (*adj*)   U3 R2
align (*v*)   U2 R2
all at once   U2 R2
all in all   U4 R2
all year round   U2 R1
alter (*v*) AWL   U7 R2
alternative (*n*) AWL   U3 R2
an extended period of time   U1 R2
an only child   U7 R1
anything but   U7 R2
apparent (*adj*) AWL   U6 R2
appreciate (*v*) AWL   U3 R2
approximate (*v*) AWL   U9 R2
aspiration (*n*)   U9 R2
at an angle   U8 R1
at random   U7 R1
at the heart of   U8 R1
at the height of one's power   U8 R1
at the same time   U6 R2
at work   U5 R2

ban (*v*)   U3 R2
be a step forward   U2 R2
be after something   U9 R2

be at a higher risk of   U2 R1
be forced to conclude   U7 R2
be known for   U1 R1
be on board with   U3 R1
be on the safe side   U9 R1
be prone to   U6 R1
be the case   U1 R2
be up to someone   U3 R2
be worth the trouble   U2 R1
beyond one's means   U6 R1
blend (*v*)   U6 R2
body of water   U4 R1
bond with (*v*)   U5 R2
brittle (*adj*)   U6 R1

captivity (*n*)   U5 R1
cater (*v*)   U4 R2
charity (*n*)   U3 R1
collapse (*v*) AWL   U1 R1
come face-to-face with   U4 R2
come into play   U7 R2
come to a similar conclusion
    U3 R1
come to mind   U4 R1
come to the realization that   U8 R2
come to the rescue   U9 R1
come with the territory   U4 R1
commit a crime   U2 R1
common sense (*n*)   U4 R1
complementary (*adj*) AWL   U7 R2
component (*n*) AWL   U8 R1
compound (*n*) AWL   U8 R1
compress (*v*)   U5 R2
conduct a study   U1 R2
confirm (*v*) AWL   U1 R2
conserve (*v*)   U2 R1
consist of (*v*)   U2 R2
consistent (*adj*) AWL   U7 R1
consumption (*n*) AWL   U2 R1
contradict (*v*) AWL   U2 R1

convert (*v*) AWL   U8 R1
convincing (*adj*) AWL   U9 R2
cross the line   U9 R2

date back to   U5 R1
death toll (*n*)   U6 R1
debate (*n*) AWL   U3 R2
defuse (*v*)   U9 R1
desperately (*adv*)   U9 R1
detect (*v*) AWL   U9 R1
diagnose (*v*)   U8 R2
discouraging (*adj*)   U6 R1
distinct (*adj*) AWL   U1 R1
do the trick   U8 R2
docile (*adj*)   U5 R2
down the road   U5 R2
draw distinctions   U7 R1
draw on (*v*)   U8 R1
drift (*v*)   U2 R2
duration (*n*) AWL   U4 R1

elaborate (*adj*)   U6 R1
element (*n*) AWL   U6 R2
elevate (*v*)   U8 R2
emerge (*v*) AWL   U4 R1
enchant (*v*)   U8 R2
end up (*v*)   U8 R2
ensure (*v*) AWL   U4 R2
entice (*v*)   U4 R2
equivalent (*adj*) AWL   U2 R1
exaggerate (*v*)   U7 R1
exhale (*v*)   U9 R1
exhibit (*v*) AWL   U8 R2
expertise (*n*) AWL   U3 R1
extended family   U6 R2

fall apart   U7 R1
fall in love with   U2 R2
fall into disrepair   U3 R1
fall to (*v*)   U3 R1

fatality (*n*)   U4 R1
feasible (*adj*)   U3 R1
filter (*v*)   U6 R2
financial (*adj*) [AWL]   U3 R1
firsthand (*adv*)   U4 R2
fit the bill   U5 R1
flaw (*n*)   U2 R2
follow suit   U2 R1
fragile (*adj*)   U4 R1
frigid (*adj*)   U4 R1
from a vantage point   U9 R1
from far and wide   U8 R1
from head to toe   U9 R2
fundamental (*adj*) [AWL]   U1 R1

get in touch with   U6 R2
get into trouble   U7 R1
give something a try   U4 R2

hand over (*v*)   U5 R2
have an advantage over   U1 R1
have an edge over   U1 R2
have an impact on   U7 R2
have something in common with
   U2 R2
have the potential   U8 R2
hazardous material   U9 R1
health food   U3 R2
how about   U4 R2
hygiene (*n*)   U8 R1

impact (*v*) [AWL]   U1 R1
in a good mood   U1 R2
in an effort to   U1 R1
in close proximity to   U5 R2
in keeping with   U6 R2
in need   U4 R2
in part   U3 R1
in shape   U1 R1
in short supply   U4 R2
in the event of   U4 R1
in the first place   U1 R1
in the presence of   U5 R1
in the wild   U5 R2
in this case   U7 R2
in this light   U3 R2

in this respect   U7 R1
in this way   U1 R2
incorporate (*v*) [AWL]   U6 R2
inflexible (*adj*) [AWL]   U5 R1
inherit (*v*)   U7 R1
inject (*v*)   U4 R2
innovative (*adj*) [AWL]   U6 R1
inspect (*v*) [AWL]   U9 R1
inspiration (*n*)   U6 R2
institute (*v*) [AWL]   U2 R2
intense (*adj*) [AWL]   U1 R2
interest (*n*)   U2 R2
isolated (*adj*) [AWL]   U7 R2
it comes as no surprise that   U8 R1

justification (*n*) [AWL]   U2 R1

keep something in mind   U6 R2
key feature   U9 R2

label (*n*) [AWL]   U7 R1
lay the foundation for   U8 R1
leap year (*n*)   U2 R2
lens (*n*)   U8 R2
living conditions (*n*)   U5 R1
lure (*n*)   U4 R1

make a proposal   U2 R1
make do with   U3 R1
make one's mark   U8 R1
make up for lost time   U2 R2
make way for   U6 R2
mandatory (*adj*)   U2 R1
manual (*n*) [AWL]   U8 R2
massive (*adj*)   U8 R1
mimic (*v*)   U9 R2
miniature (*adj*)   U9 R2
motivation (*n*) [AWL]   U1 R2

no matter what   U2 R1
not . . . at all   U1 R1
not a single   U4 R1
not stand a chance of   U6 R1
nothing beats   U4 R1

obesity (*n*)   U7 R2

oblivious (*adj*)   U9 R1
obstacle (*n*)   U3 R1
occupant (*n*) [AWL]   U6 R1
offspring (*n*)   U5 R2
on a national scale   U2 R1
on one's own   U7 R1
on the cutting edge   U7 R2
on the market   U1 R1
optimal (*adj*)   U1 R2
option (*n*) [AWL]   U4 R1
out of harm's way   U9 R1
out of service   U4 R2
over the years   U1 R1

pad of paper   U8 R2
paradox (*n*)   U9 R2
participate (*v*) [AWL]   U3 R1
pass something on to   U7 R2
patronize (*v*)   U4 R2
pave the way for   U5 R1
pay off (*v*)   U6 R1
peer group (*n*)   U7 R1
persistent (*adj*) [AWL]   U1 R2
phase (*n*) [AWL]   U7 R1
play a role in   U1 R2
portable (*adj*)   U3 R2
positive feedback   U1 R2
potential (*adj*) [AWL]   U5 R2
practical application   U8 R2
precise (*adj*) [AWL]   U2 R2
prison sentence   U2 R2
promote (*v*) [AWL]   U2 R1
pros and cons   U3 R2
prosperity (*n*)   U5 R1
protest (*v*)   U9 R2
put something to the test   U9 R2

quench one's thirst   U3 R2
quit (*v*)   U8 R2

radical (*adj*) [AWL]   U7 R2
reinforced (*adj*) [AWL]   U1 R1
remote (*adj*)   U9 R1
resilient (*adj*)   U6 R1
rest on the shoulders of   U9 R1
revolution (*n*) [AWL]   U2 R2

rule out (*v*)   U5 R1
run out of (*v*)   U4 R1
running water   U3 R1

safeguard (*n*)   U6 R1
sanitation (*n*)   U3 R1
say nothing of   U6 R1
scan (*v*)   U9 R1
sensation (*n*)   U1 R2
shift (*n*) AWL   U5 R1
solar (*adj*)   U2 R2
solely (*adv*) AWL   U5 R2
some sort of   U8 R2
spare parts   U3 R1
sparingly (*adv*)   U3 R1
spend one's life   U9 R2
sphere (*n*) AWL   U8 R2
stability (*n*) AWL   U1 R2

steer clear of   U4 R2
strategy (*n*) AWL   U1 R2
stress (*n*) AWL   U7 R2
subsequent (*adj*) AWL   U7 R1
suppress (*v*)   U7 R2
sustain (*v*) AWL   U8 R1

tackle (*v*)   U8 R1
take sides   U3 R2
take up space   U3 R2
talent (*n*)   U7 R1
temporary (*adj*) AWL   U7 R1
terrain (*n*)   U1 R1
these days   U8 R2
thrill (*n*)   U4 R1
tone of voice   U5 R2
trace (*v*) AWL   U1 R1
trait (*n*)   U5 R2

transfer (*v*) AWL   U1 R1
transformation (*n*) AWL   U5 R1
transport (*v*) AWL   U3 R2
turn of the century   U6 R2
turn out to be   U5 R2

untangle (*v*)   U7 R2
update (*v*)   U6 R2

valid (*adj*) AWL   U2 R1
ventilation (*n*)   U6 R2
version (*n*) AWL   U9 R2
vibrant (*adj*)   U8 R1
vigorous (*adj*)   U3 R2
volunteer (*n*) AWL   U4 R2

withstand (*v*)   U6 R1
worst of all   U3 R2

CREDITS

Text Sources

The following sources were consulted when writing the readings for *Reading and Vocabulary Focus 3*.

6–8: "Running Barefoot Reduces Stress—On Feet" by Richard A. Lovett: http://news.nationalgeographic.com/news/2010/01/100127-barefoot-running-better-impact/; **16–17:** "Runner's High Hardwired in People—And Dogs" by Christine Dell'Amore: http://news.nationalgeographic.com/news/2012/05/120510-runners-high-evolution-people-dogs-science/; additional source: "The Evolution of the Runner's High" by Gretchen Reynolds: http://well.blogs.nytimes.com/2012/04/25/the-evolution-of-the-runners-high/; **28–30:** "Daylight Saving Time 2012: Why and When Does It Begin?" by Brian Handwerk: http://news.nationalgeographic.com/news/2012/12/120309-daylight-savings-time-2012-what-time-is-it-spring-forward-nation/; additional source: "Seize the Daylight" by David Prerau (2005). New York: Thunder's Mouth Press; **38–40:** "Leap Year: How the World Makes Up for Lost Time" by Brian Handwerk: http://news.nationalgeographic.com/news/2008/02/080228-leap-year.html; **52–54:** "The Burden of Thirst" by Tina Rosenberg: http://ngm.nationalgeographic.com/2010/04/water-slaves/rosenberg-text; additional source: "Can Matt Damon Bring Clean Water to Africa?": http://www.fastcompany.com/1760918/can-matt-damon-bring-clean-water-africa; **62–63:** "The Big Thirst" by Charles Fishman (2011). New York: The Free Press; additional source: "Bottled Water is a Big Drain": http://www.businessweek.com/debateroom/archives/2008/06/bottled_water_i.html; **74–77:** "Dream Trip: Dive the Poles" by Eric Sala: http://adventure.nationalgeographic.com/adventure/trips/bucket-list/dive-the-poles/; additional source: "Extreme Cave Diving": http://www.pbs.org/wgbh/nova/earth/extreme-cave-diving.html; **84–85:** "Disaster Strikes and I Still Go" by Daisann McClain: http://travel.nationalgeographic.com/travel/traveler-magazine/real-travel/disasters/; **96–98:** "Nature: Holy Cow": http://www.pbs.org/wnet/nature/episodes/holy-cow/introduction/1812/; **106–107:** "Taming the Wild" by Evan Ratliff: http://ngm.nationalgeographic.com/2011/03/taming-wild-animals/ratliff-text; **118–120:** "Safe Houses": http://ngm.nationalgeographic.com/big-idea/10/earthquakes; **128–130:** "An Architect's Vision: Bare Elegance in China" by Jane Perlez: http://www.nytimes.com/2012/08/12/arts/design/wang-shu-of-china-advocates-sustainable-architecture.html?pagewanted=all&_r=0; additional source: "In Vietnam, A Traditional House Goes Green" by Mike Ives: http://www.time.com/time/magazine/article/0,9171,1952313,00.html; **142–143:** "Siblings share genes, but rarely personality" by Alix Spiegel: http://www.npr.org/2010/11/18/131424595/siblings-share-genes-but-rarely-personalities; **150–152:** "A Thing or Two about Twins" by Peter Miller: http://ngm.nationalgeographic.com/2012/01/twins/miller-text; additional source: "Why DNA is not your destiny" by John Cloud: http://www.time.com/time/magazine/article/0,9171,1952313,00.html; **164–166:** "1001 inventions: The enduring legacy of Muslim civilization" by Salim Al-Hassani, Ed. (2012). Washington D.C.: National Geographic; additional source: "What the ancients did for us: Islamic civilization": BBC; **174–176:** "Fold Everything": http://ngm.nationalgeographic.com/big-idea/03/origami; **188–190:** "Could Cyborg Cockroaches Save Your Life?" by Amanda Fiegl: http://news.nationalgeographic.com/news/2012/09/120907-cyborg-cockroaches-video-science-remote-control-robots-bugs/; additional source: "Danger Robots": http://science.discovery.com/tv-shows/science-channel-presents/videos/discoveries-this-week-danger-robots.htm; **198–200:** "Us. And Them" by Chris Carroll: http://ngm.nationalgeographic.com/2011/08/robots/carroll-text

Art Credits

Cover: GARDEL Bertrand.fr/Getty Images; **iii:** (t) REUTERS/Sergio Perez; **iii:** (c) YouraPechkin/E+/Getty Images; **iii:** (b) DESMOND BOYLAN/Reuters/Corbis; **iv:** (t) Tyler Roemer; **iv:** (c) Michael Nichols/National Geographic Creative; **iv:** (b) Jino Lee/National Geographic Creative; **v:** (t) Biophoto Associates/Photo Researchers/Getty Images; **v:** (c) REUTERS/China Photos ASW; **v:** (b) WANG ZHAO/

AFP/Getty Images; **vi:** (t) Jino Lee/National Geographic Creative; **vi:** (b) David L. Ryan/Lonely Planet Images/Getty Images; **vii:** Bryan Christie/National Geographic Creative; **viii:** Alison Wright/National Geographic Creative; **ix:** Ken Wilson-Max/Alamy; **2–3:** REUTERS/Sergio Perez; **4–5:** Ben Horton/National Geographic Creative; **6–7:** Aurora Photos/Alamy; **6:** (bl) Robb Kendrick/National Geographic Creative; **7:** (cr) Serenethos/Fotolia; **7:** (br) Llike/Fotolia; **8:** (bl) Michel Tcherevkoff/Stone/Getty Images; **8:** (br) Hugh Threlfall/Alamy; **11:** Aurora Photos/Alamy; **13:** Jordan Siemens/Iconica/Getty Images; **14–15:** Rich Reid/National Geographic Creative; **16–17:** (t) Frans Lanting/National Geographic Image Creative; **16:** (tr) Matthias Breiter/National Geographic Creative; **17:** PetStockBoys/Alamy; **22:** Jim Rogash/Stringer/Getty Images; **24–25:** YouraPechkin/E+/Getty Images; **26–27:** Alexey Gromov/AFP/Getty Images; **28:** Topical Press Agency/Getty Images; **29:** Paul Chesley/National Geographic Creative; **32:** Panoramic Images/National Geographic Creative; **35:** Niday Picture Library/Alamy; **36–37:** Jim Richardson/National Geographic Creative; **38:** Yiannis Papadimitriou/Shutterstock; **39:** JACOPIN BSIP/SuperStock; **40:** DEA/G. DAGLI ORTI/De Agostini/Getty Images; **45:** LOOK Die Bildagentur der Fotografen GmbH/Alamy; **46:** (tc) Peter Horree/Alamy; **48–49:** DESMOND BOYLAN/Reuters/Corbis; **50–51:** PETER ESSICK/National Geographic Image Collection; **52:** Lynn Johnson/National Geographic Creative; **54:** Tommy Trenchard/Alamy; **58:** Mauricio Handler/National Geographic Creative; **60–61:** Jason Edwards/National Geographic Creative; **62:** david pearson/Alamy; **63:** Philip and Karen Smith/Iconica/Getty Images; **67:** Javier Larrea/age fotostock/Getty Images; **69:** mtkang/Fotolia; **70–71:** Tyler Roemer; **72–73:** Paul Nicklen/National Geographic Creative; **74–75:** Reinhard Dirscherl/Alamy; **75:** Jens Kuhfs/Photographer's Choice/Getty Images; **76:** Yvette Cardozo/Photolibrary/Getty Images; **77:** Brian J. Skerry/National Geographic/Getty Images; **82–83:** REUTERS/Tony Gentile; **84:** (tc) Jim Reed/Science Faction/Getty Images; **84:** (tl) Jim West/Alamy; **92–93:** Michael Nichols/National Geographic Creative; **94–95:** Kuntal Josher; **96–97:** Frans Lanting/National Geographic Creative; **97:** NGM Art/National Geographic Creative; **98:** Ray Roberts/Alamy; **103:** Anne-Marie Palmer/Alamy; **104–105:** Melissa Farlow/National Geographic Creative; **106:** Stockbyte/Getty Images; **113:** (tl) Joel Sartore/National Geographic Creative; **113:** (tr) Farlap/Alamy; **113:** (cl) Steve Raymer/National Geographic Creative; **113:** (cr) C-images/Alamy; **113:** (bl) Thomas Kitchin & Victoria Hurst/All Canada Photos/Getty Images; **113:** (br) blickwinkel/Alamy; **115–116:** Jino Lee/National Geographic Creative; **116–117:** David L. Ryan/Lonely Planet Images/Getty Images; **118–119:** Bryan Christie/National Geographic Creative; **120:** NGM Maps/National Geographic Creative; **124:** Alison Wright/National Geographic Creative; **126–127:** Klaus Lang/All Canada Photos/Getty Images; **128:** (bl) Iconotec/Alamy; **128:** (br) REUTERS/Stringer; **129:** VIEW Pictures Ltd/Alamy; **130:** Marla Holden/Alamy; **132:** SFL Travel/Alamy; **135:** Paul Macleod/National Geographic Creative; **136:** Ken Wilson-Max/Alamy; **138–139:** Biophoto Associates/Photo Researchers/Getty Images; **140–141:** Alex Treadway/National Geographic Creative; **142:** Jaguar PS/Shutterstock; **145:** Chris Walter/WireImage/Getty Images; **148–149:** Alison Wright/National Geographic; **150–151:** National Geographic Image Collection/Alamy; **152:** Lawson Parker/National Geographic Creative; **154:** Ron Kuntz/AFP/Getty Images; **157:** Teh Eng Koon/AFP/Getty Images; **158:** Wathiq Khuzaie/Getty Images; **160–161:** REUTERS/China Photos ASW; **162–163:** DeAgostini/Getty Images; **164–165:** Eliot Elisofon//Time Life Pictures/Getty Images; **168:** chrisdorney/Fotolia; **172–173:** Rebecca Hale/National Geographic Creative; **174:** Don Farrall/Photodisc/Getty Images; **175:** Rod Hyde/Lawrence Livermore National Laboratory; **178:** Shaul Schwarz/Getty Images; **180–181:** Andrew Paterson/Alamy; **183:** Thomas Lohnes/AFP/Getty Images; **184–185:** WANG ZHAO/AFP/Getty Images; **186–187:** FREDRIK PERSSON/AFP/Getty Images; **188:** Yoshikazu Tsuno/AFP/Getty Images; **189:** (tr) Art Directors & TRIP/Alamy; **189:** (bl) Splash News/Newscom; **190:** iBionicS Lab/North Carolina State University; **195:** Toru Yamanaka/AFP/Getty Images; **196–197:** Richard Nowitz/National Geographic Creative; **198:** Yoshikazu Tsuno/AFP/Getty Images; **199:** Yoshikazu Tsuno/AFP/Getty Images; **200:** REUTERS/Reuters Photographer; **205:** Yoshikazu Tsuno/AFP/Getty Images; **206:** Imagno/Hulton Archive/Getty Images